WOUNDED
HEARTS

WOUNDED HEARTS

Memories of the Halifax Protestant Orphans' Home

Lois Legge

NIMBUS
PUBLISHING LTD.
— NIMBUS.CA —

Nimbus Publishing Limited
3660 Strawberry Hill Street, Halifax, NS, B3K 5A9
(902) 455-4286 nimbus.ca

Printed and bound in Canada
NB1397

Design: Jenn Embree
Editor: Angela Mombourquette

Library and Archives Canada Cataloguing in Publication

Title: Wounded hearts : memories of the Halifax Protestant Orphans' Home / Lois Legge.
Names: Legge, Lois, author.
Description: Includes bibliographical references.
Identifiers: Canadiana 20190156899 |
ISBN 9781771087957 (softcover)
Subjects: LCSH: Halifax Protestant Orphans' Home—History. |
LCSH: Orphanages—Nova Scotia—Halifax—History.
Classification: LCC HV1010.H352 H35 2019 |
DDC 362.73/2—dc23

Nimbus Publishing acknowledges the financial support for its publishing activities from the Government of Canada, the Canada Council for the Arts, and from the Province of Nova Scotia. We are pleased to work in partnership with the Province of Nova Scotia to develop and promote our creative industries for the benefit of all Nova Scotians.

For Richard and Chelsea:
my heart, my home.

Contents

Preface 1

Introduction: "Little Wanderers and Little Outcasts" 5

Chapter One: Scarred – Shirley Carter 25

Chapter Two: Heartbreak Songs – Linda Gray-LeBlanc 51

Chapter Three: Better Than Home – Leonard Chater
and Joe Gooey 71

Chapter Four: The Fortunate One – Sandy Murray 95

Chapter Five: "One Boy" – Paul Sabarots 119

Chapter Six: Number 11 – James Underwood 143

Chapter Seven: Redemption – Elaine McLellan 165

Chapter Eight: "I Want My Story Told" – "Margaret" 183

Chapter Nine: A Safe Place – Veith House 189

Chapter Ten: Return 201

Afterword: The Records Speak 211

Acknowledgements 227

Note on Sources 229

PREFACE

"It is because I think so much of warm and sensitive hearts that I would spare them from being wounded."

– Charles Dickens, *Oliver Twist*

I FIRST HEARD ABOUT THE Halifax Protestant Orphans' Home from a reporter who was covering old bones.

Construction workers had found the remains while digging up a section of North Park Street and archeologists thought they might have been from a child. It had been the first site of what was later known as the Halifax Protestant Orphanage, founded in 1857 and closed in 1970. Forensic experts eventually determined they were animal bones, not the skeletons of children who had once lived in this forgotten place from another time.

Interest died down, and I tucked the story idea away for another day.

But hidden things often rise up—or never go away, as I've learned again and again from the former residents of this Halifax institution who were often beaten by staff members who scared them and taught them, as one person put it, "about the uncertainty of life."

Today these former residents are senior citizens whose sons and daughters are grown, and whose grandchildren are growing or are about to be born.

But as I listened to them speak, I thought of them as children. I thought of their baby pictures and school photographs and old black-and-white snapshots taken inside the orphanage—a place for children who were neglected or abused at home, or whose parents had died, or whose parents were too sick or too poor to raise them. I remembered ringlets rimming tiny faces, and gap-toothed smiles. I remembered little bowties, worn for first communion, and tiny hands holding stuffed toys.

I wondered how anyone could ever strap them or keep them in closets or tie them to beds, as many say some of the matrons—the women who ran the orphanage—often did. I wondered how their parents or their foster parents could have beaten them or starved them or humiliated them, as some say their blood relatives and appointed guardians did.

I wondered how those who had been loved but had lost their parents to poverty or sickness or death had managed in this strange place of loneliness and fear.

And I wondered, after all of that, how they went on to build careers and loving families, and how they formed compassionate hearts out of the wreckage of their own.

It's a daunting task to take someone's life story into your own hands and try to tell it with truth and dignity and compassion—and to do it without adding to the hurt. But thinking about their lives as children made me determined to try.

And made me hope, in some small way, to help heal these wounded hearts of long ago.

Introduction:
"Little Wanderers
and Little Outcasts"

T HE NAMES APPEAR LIKE PHANTOMS on
paper, buried deep in tattered records from another time.

Bess Hooper, seven–died of unknown causes in 1859.

Sarah Churley, twelve–died of "some affection of the brain"
in 1876.

Five children, unnamed–died of diphtheria in 1880.

Other orphanage "inmates" emerge as numbers–admitted
or discharged, "adopted or claimed."

Some of the Halifax Protestant Orphans' Home's past is
long lost, stored only in the memories of survivors. Some of it
is incomplete–details missing among these yellowed records,
in faded folders, tied with string.

This photo of Halifax Protestant Orphanage founder Robert Uniacke hangs in the former orphanage building that is now known as Veith House. *(Author photo)*

The collection of annual reports, financial records, meeting minutes, letters, and handwritten notes—stored at Nova Scotia Archives—includes sanitized or mundane versions of a time former residents describe as far more sinister. Although occasionally, in later orphanage records, glimpses of a darker reality also emerge.

The oldest of the documents are frayed now. And faded.

So fragile they can't be photographed or photocopied.

So thin they sometimes crumble to the touch.

Most veil as much as they reveal about the "little waifs" who were "snatched as brands from the burning" and rescued by "their Heavenly Father's love."

What happened to these children—"little wanderers and little outcasts"—in the days of paupers and poor houses, of orphanages and asylums, of pity and piety?

No one will ever know. Most of their stories aren't written down or remembered.

But for the founder of the privately run institution—overseen by an all-male board of governors and the "Ladies' Committee"; staffed by all-powerful "matrons"—it's a different story.

꿍 ◎ ꩜

ROBERT FITZGERALD UNIACKE

BY MOST ACCOUNTS, Robert Fitzgerald Uniacke was a kindly pastor who dedicated his life to helping the poor—especially poor children.

Whatever became of his orphanage later on, his intentions appear to have been good, if tinged by the evangelical fires of his faith and the traditions of the times.

Old records portray a man who worked tirelessly on behalf of those less fortunate than himself, including the adults he ministered and the children who eventually ended up in his orphanage.

He took over as pastor of St. George's Church, a congregation that then encompassed a wide geographical area of Halifax, in 1825, and he remained until his death in 1870.

During that time, according to archival accounts, he displayed an unwavering dedication to the task—from leading decades-long expansions to his parish, to building schools for the poor, to founding other churches, and, eventually, to founding the orphanage.

As Canon Henry Ward Cunningham—the rector of St. George's in the early 1900s—writes in his *History of St. George's Church*, Uniacke's ministry went well beyond the church. He tended to the poor and the sick, in a time and in a city often plagued by poverty and deadly disease.

"In 1834, Halifax was visited by the dreaded Cholera," Cunningham writes in a lengthy manuscript, published as a series of articles over several years, in the church's magazine.

> Most people who could do so left the city but not thus did Mr. and Mrs. Uniacke forsake the sick and suffering, but remained at their posts, nursing, giving medicine, soothing the sufferer, comforting the dying.
>
> ...When the smallpox visited Halifax he turned the Rectory into a hospital and his stable into a medicine supply and clothing and bedding were given freely to all who needed them. He was both physician and nurse.

Uniacke came from a wealthy family of lawyers and judges—even a Nova Scotia premier. But he was also a strong proponent of education for the poor. Archival documents show he repeatedly sought, and received, government money to fund his schools, which catered to poor children of all denominations.

By the mid-1800s he and other prominent citizens, including prolific philanthropist Isabella Binney Cogswell, were seeking support for an orphanage, one of many in Halifax's history.

The so-called "Orphan House"—built in the 1700s, and by historical accounts a run-down, rat-infested facility—preceded it. Other orphanages and homes for poor children followed, including St.

Joseph's Orphanage (a Catholic facility), St. Patrick's Home for Boys (also Catholic), the Halifax Infants' Home (a Protestant institution), The Home of the Guardian Angel (Catholic), and the Nova Scotia Home for Colored Children. Other institutions were a combination of orphanage and reformatory.

Halifax also housed the destitute in institutions like the Halifax County Poors' Farm—for "paupers" and "the harmless insane"—which opened in 1887. It later became the Halifax County Home and Mental Hospital.

Perhaps the most notorious institution of them all was a children's reform school known as the Halifax Industrial School (see page 217), which historian Renée Lafferty-Salhany says was by far the worst children's facility she came across while writing her 2012 book, *The Guardianship of Best Interests: Institutional Care for the Children of the Poor in Halifax 1850–1960.*

These nineteenth- and early twentieth-century institutions were of a time when society was starkly divided, says the author, by religion and by race, by rich and by poor. And they were also of a time when poor children, who often ended up in the orphanage, were not only pitied as unfortunate outcasts, but were also feared.

"These would definitely be children who were on the margins of society; these are poor kids. The ideals are kids who are kind of fat, plump little cherubic things, and definitely white," Lafferty-Salhany, who is also a history professor at Brock University in St. Catharines, Ontario, says in an interview.

But poor children, both black and white, were considered a potential menace to society.

"There's a big concern...that when you have kids that are poor, kids that are undisciplined,...[that] they were going to grow up to become criminals and burdens on the state, so you wanted to put them in these institutions to train them for what they considered...a useful life."

And as residents of the Protestant home would discover, this training often included harsh discipline or even manual labour when they were sent out to work as indentured servants.

❧❦❧

THE MONEY TRAIL

FROM THE BEGINNING, a group of well-to-do Halifax citizens had helped Robert Uniacke raise money for the facility, which was known as the "Orphanage Asylum" during the fundraising stage. They also sat on the first, and subsequent, board of governors. William Cunard, son of shipping magnate Samuel Cunard, was an early and long-time board president. According to one orphanage document, he personally raised $16,497 for the running of the home. He also continued to contribute annually to the institution for many years—$50 or $100 during the time when the home was on North Park Street and its annual operating costs hovered around $2,000.

Doctors, judges, lawyers, and ministers made up the all-male board of governors, and they funded the institution in annual installments of ten, twenty, fifty, or seventy-five dollars. Other citizens chipped in between one and four dollars a year. Wealthy Halifax women, often board members' wives, served on the Ladies' Committee, which oversaw the operation of the home and fundraised as well.

The Protestant Orphans' Home on North Park Street in 1874; almost eighty children passed through the home that year. *(Nova Scotia Archives)*

These types of contributions continued years later when the home moved to its first Veith Street location, which was destroyed in the 1917 Halifax Explosion. By 1924, at its final location on the same street, the orphanage was still primarily funded by the facility's board of governors and wealthy benefactors. As they had in the 1800s, parents who directly placed children there occasionally contributed small amounts.

Bequests and fundraising also aided the institution, as did a long-running money source known as The Murdock Fund, named after William Murdock, a wealthy banking magnate who had been on the orphanage's board of governors in 1859, and who had left legacies to a host of Halifax institutions.

Off and on through the years, the City of Halifax contributed grants to the institution as well, but the provincial government became a core funder—and one of the most consistent sources of financial support—from the early twentieth century on, and its funding grew substantially over time, as did its placement of so-called "wards"—children under government care.

Records show that for many years, the province was second only to the board's wealthy members as the primary source of funding.

As the years passed, the number of children placed there by the provincial government and various children's aid societies rose too.

"It seems that the department of welfare [DCW] is getting more children than CAS [Children's Aid Society] and most of the cases coming to us now are coming from the department," notes a 1959 monthly Ladies' Committee report.

Many handwritten notes also mention the "excellent cooperation" between these agencies and the orphanage, which, despite these close ties, still operated without the province's supervision and had complete day-to-day control over the children.

This arrangement would turn out to be a key question for some former residents, who wonder why—given the province's financial support—they were left to the mercy of the matrons, whose cruelty, they say, has left lifelong emotional scars.

MIDDLE-CLASS MORALIZERS

The well-off citizens of the early twentieth century tended to look down on those who were less financially stable. Any sense of altruism was tinged with a sense of moral superiority and stereotypes about race and

Children gather in a common room at the Protestant Orphanage in 1918. *(Nova Scotia Archives)*

class. That reasoning—with an accompanying tone of condescension—is illustrated in some of Ernest Blois's writings about the conditions and the people of "this class."

Blois was supervisor of the Department of Neglected and Delinquent Children when he described several "typical cases" in his 1919 annual report—a revealing look into how poor people, or people with disabilities—called "defective"—or non-white people were perceived by those Lafferty-Salhany calls "middle-class moralizers."

"A familiar sight in certain quarters of the city for some years has been a boy and girl of eight and ten years, dirty, ill-clad, under-nourished, cross-eyed, veritable little street Arabs with 'sub-normal' written all over them," he writes. "They have an awful heritage, every form of mental and physical defect on the father's side and tuberculosis and alcoholism on the mother's.

"These children are the inevitable result of such a union and such a home—a few crowded evil smelling rooms

in a mouldy tenement. Our effort to place the girl in the
I.O.D.E. Home met with violent opposition on the part of
the parents. The mother was a pathetic sight. Her grief was
like that of an animal being deprived of her young and her
grasp of the situation equally intelligent."

She was eventually "converted" he says, after seeing
the I.O.D.E. Home "bathed in sunshine" and evidence of
its "love and comfort."

"The boy is still at large. One day he is seen dragged
from under the wheels of an automobile, the next he is
selling papers and bruised and buffeted by the ruffian who
robs him. Unfortunately he is one of many. There is no
place for him, but ultimately, the poor house or the jail."

Authorities saw the orphanages and the reform schools
and other children's institutions as ways to prevent the
"the cultural contamination" they feared could "infect
good children," Lafferty-Salhany says.

They could tell themselves that it was for the good of
the "orphans," the "delinquents," the "cripples," the
"feeble-minded," and the wayward girls and women—and
their offspring—who were also a concern for the people
running the orphanages, and the people funding them.

❧◦❧

"CHRISTIAN PRINCIPLES"

RELIGION WAS CLOSELY tied to the institution from the start and is a key and unrelenting reference in reports that remain.

In the early years of the orphanage, the children attended St. George's Church every Sunday, and according to one orphanage document, "special seats were built for them in front of the pews. The Rev. Mr. Uniacke was pastor." The children received in-house Sunday school instruction as well.

The Ladies' Committee said a prayer and read a Bible passage at the beginning of each monthly meeting. Their stated philosophy, along with providing shelter, food, and education, was to immerse the children in "Christian principles"—in preparation for life and death.

"There are now many good, honest and industrious young men and women who owe their present condition to the existence of this Institution," they wrote in their 1879 annual report.

> When it is remembered under what circumstances, for the most part, the children are taken in, the change which is effected is the more remarkable.... Whilst the religious instruction which is instilled into them is so valuable in its effects, these children whose earthly course would evitably be downwards to the lowest depths of moral

degradation, are "snatched as brands from the burning" to get a fair start for a good life with a knowledge of their Heavenly Father's love, and of their Savior Jesus Christ.

...The very name "orphan" tells of the helpless and uncared for condition, and thus it is that the most solemn charge is laid upon all to be considerate of this class of their fellow-creatures.

The Ladies' Committee of that era often sent orphanage children to live with adoptive or foster parents, requiring only a positive letter from their minister beforehand. Several reports cite glowing letters from adoptive parents and adopted children about how they had been brought up, with only occasional hints that all was not well for everyone, and they are all anonymous voices in the void: the children's stories are told under the watchful eye or through the filters of their adult guardians—the Ladies' Committee, their foster or adoptive parents, or the people to whom they were indentured.

"The committee have been much cheered by the receipt of several very satisfactory letters concerning children adopted, among them one from a clergyman who adopted a little girl twelve years ago, in which he speaks of her as being a good, kind, Christian girl," the committee writes in 1881, a year in which seventeen of the children were adopted.

"They are in nearly all cases adopted as members of the family, and treated as such, loving and beloved," they say in 1888.

EXPLOITATION VERSUS PROTECTION

THE GUARDIANS OF the orphanage and other institutions considered discipline, along with religious training—and in some cases, manual labour that would lead to menial jobs—a key part of their mission. Some children were indentured, apparently sent to work for the families and institutions that took them in. This was "very common" in the nineteenth century, says historian Lafferty-Salhany.

"One of the real faults of both foster care and institutions is that whatever they thought they were doing, in the end,...really what they were looking to do was find cheap labour," she says.

"St. Paul's Home for Girls was training them to become domestic servants; they'd take in laundry to raise money, washing curtains of well-to-do folks in Halifax, so...it's very much in the economic interests of the city, of the institutions, of the foster parents to find kids to do cheap labour."

It became less common as the century closed, and authorities started, at least in theory, to understand that children should be protected rather than exploited.

"If they're doing it [by that time], they're not admitting that they're doing it," Lafferty-Salhany says—a key distinction, given the experiences of kids who were essentially put to work by foster parents all the way up to the 1950s.

Bylaws adopted by the Protestant orphanage around 1886 stipulated that "in case of the decease of those by whom the child may be adopted, or upon its receiving any unkind and cruel treatment, inconsistent with terms of indenture, the Ladies reserve to themselves the right of resuming control over the children."

It isn't clear if, or how often, that happened. Almost universally, the former residents who've shared their stories here stress that authorities never personally asked how they were treated either inside or outside the orphanage.

꒰ ◎ ꒱

THE MATRONS

INSIDE THE ORPHANAGE, the head matron had complete control over how the children were treated, as did other matrons, until the institution closed in 1970.

The Ladies' Committee spelled out the matrons' duties in 1883. Among them:

"Full control of the children except during school hours."

"To see that the children are always kept clean, that they are bathed twice a week, that their heads are regularly combed (combing to be done in the bathroom) and that their clothes are made and kept in order."

"To have the bedding changed every Saturday morning."

To be "very particular in attending to their habits, morals and manners...always being present with them at their meals, and see that they behave themselves properly."

To visit the children's rooms every night "to see that everything is safe and comfortable."

The head matron and her husband were also required to attend church with the children every Sunday and to ensure they were trained "in the knowledge and love of the Lord Jesus Christ." She was allowed one afternoon and evening off a week.

If a child's parents were alive, they had no say in how the children were treated, as noted in the home's constitution and bylaws of 1886: "No parent, guardian, or other person not officially connected with the institution shall interfere in any manner with the care or management of children while they remain in the home."

Children at the Protestant Orphanage learned this again and again as the years passed and matrons came and went. Most of the matrons now long gone.

༄৩ ⊕ ঙ৲৩

A NEW BUILDING

THE ORPHANAGE BEGAN on North Park Street. But eventually the Ladies' Committee pushed for a bigger building, in part to help stop the spread of diseases, and that led to the move to the first of two buildings the orphanage eventually occupied on Veith Street, within sight of Halifax Harbour.

"At present it is almost impossible to prevent diseases of an infectious and contagious character from spreading rapidly, and the necessity for better means of isolation must be evident to all who consider the character of the institution," the committee wrote in 1874.

"Owing to the presence of the fever in the spring, so much inconvenience was experienced that the committee felt the necessity of representing the matter strongly to the governors and expressing it as their unanimous opinion that some prompt action should be taken with regard to it."

The board and the committee eventually settled on buying a home that was at that time owned by one William Jordan, Esq.

"The house is large and airy, having an excellent basement and has been built with much care and expense," the Ladies wrote in their 1875 annual report. "The grounds are extensive," they noted. And a large playground ensures children "can get plenty of air and exercise without having to go outside of the confines of the institution."

In the following year's reports, they are reveling in their new premises and the fact it is "wonderfully free from epidemic disease"–"remarkable," they say, "considering the character of the institution, or age and class of the children....

"During the year several improvements have been carried out regarding sanitary arrangements, and it may now be safely said that no building could have better guarantees of health and purity."

But that was about to change.

꽃 ⊙ ꬺ

THE HALIFAX EXPLOSION

ONE OF THE biggest milestones in the home's history arrived in a flash and a fury when the Halifax Explosion—the largest man-made explosion the world had ever known—tore through the north end of the city.

"On this site the Protestant Orphans' Home stood until December 6th, 1917," says a plaque that sits just a few steps away from the site. "On that fateful day the Halifax Explosion destroyed the orphanage along with nearly every other house on Veith Street.

"A story is told that after hearing the minor detonations that preceded the Halifax Explosion, the matron gathered twenty-six children and two staff in the orphanage basement. She thought the city was being bombed. Miraculously, when the building collapsed and burned after the catastrophic blast, seven children survived."

This monument marks the destruction of the first Veith St. location of the Protestant Orphans' Home during the Halifax Explosion. (*Author photo*)

The head matron, identified in newspaper clippings as Mary Knaut, died in the blast, as did assistant matron Ethel Melvin, housemaid Lena Meagher, and many of the children— who authorities said burned to death or were never found.

But it's not clear, despite the plaque, exactly how many children survived. The numbers vary in different accounts. A 1919 letter from the Protestant Home's secretary, M. Scott, outlines the challenges the institution faced in the aftermath.

"This home is striving to rise from its ashes, and amid many difficulties continues its work," the secretary writes in the home's yearly overview, contained in the 1919 Journals of the House of Assembly.

> The terrible disaster of December 6th wiped this Home out of existence. Of the forty-one children then in the Home fifteen only survived the disaster. A temporary Home was secured in the extreme south end of the City, and in April 1918 the work was again taken up. This house is not suitable either in situation or accommodation and the matron has been handicapped in many ways.
>
> ...It is hoped in the near future a site may be secured.

By 1924 the home had been rebuilt in the north end, in a new building on the same street. That building is now a community centre known as Veith House.

The former orphanage building is now Veith House, a community hub that provides services for low-income children and adults in Halifax's north end. (*Author photo*)

❧ ◦ ☙

END OF AN INSTITUTION

THE LAST OF the children left that building in 1970 after Nova Scotia followed a North America–wide wave of de-institutionalization in favour of foster care—although that too, as the experiences of so many former orphanage residents can attest, was fraught with problems. Once again, authorities were "dealing a lot with the honour system," says historian Lafferty-Salhany, meaning that foster parents were not held accountable for the care of the children. "And a lot of kids end up suffering."

The depths of those kids' suffering, in orphanages and elsewhere, was also becoming more widely understood, and there was a growing consensus about the psychological damage caused by institutionalization itself.

"Even where deliberate abuse was not in evidence," Lafferty-Salhany writes in *The Guardianship of Best Interests*, "and where institutional staffs provided adequate and loving care for their charges, psychologists, doctors, and child welfare specialists have condemned the effects of institutionalization on the psychological and emotional well-being of children."

Researchers were also learning about the widespread damage physical and emotional abuse can have on the body and on the mind, increasing the risk of everything from heart disease to depression.

Former resident Shirley Carter puts it simply: "It will last."

Chapter One:
Scarred
Shirley Carter

S HIRLEY CARTER'S MEMORIES RISE IN waves of terror.

She's tied to her bed.

She smells smoke.

She panics as her sister tries to help.

Maybe I will have to burn to this bed so they will be exposed, Shirley thinks, as her sister, who has an intellectual disability, struggles to untie the knots that still bind her to her childhood. *I may have to lose my life to save all these other kids.*

Shirley was six or seven then. She's almost eighty now, but she can't forget.

All the nights she lay tied to her bed.

All the days she stood in closets..

All the years she felt leather straps striking her skin.

She can't breathe. Her heart races as she goes back to the place of hurt and humiliation—to the indignities that have consumed her life.

Her voice trembles as she talks about it over the telephone from her Ontario home—in 2016 and 2018—unburdening herself of memories she has never shared before. A purging of the past that eventually helps her in the present.

But on this day in 2016, the past is nothing but pain.

"I think about it all the time," says the mother of three, grandmother of five, great-grandmother of nine, whose mind and body has, for so long, been "all tied up in knots."

This retired nurse's orphanage story begins even before she can remember. She was just a toddler when her parents placed her and two of her siblings in the Halifax Protestant Orphan's Home. She lived there until she was eleven, raised by the matrons she says abused her.

Shirley Carter, in the only photo she owns of herself as a baby. She was placed in the orphanage as a toddler, but doesn't remember that time. *(Shirley Carter)*

In her only baby picture, Shirley is laughing, clutching a stuffed toy. She likes to imagine the matrons doted on her then, a blonde, rosy-cheeked two-year-old.

But she knows that might be wishful thinking.

"God knows what happened to me before I could remember....It might have been very traumatic," she says.

"The better part of me wants to think they were so happy to have a little baby in there....I don't want to think they were abusing me at two years old. I don't want to think they were hitting me at two years old."

But that did come later. Day after day. Year after year, in a facility its founders called a "peaceful and happy home" for children "who might otherwise be left uncared for, exposed to every temptation and sin, fatherless and friendless in a cold world."

Perhaps it was peaceful and happy for some. But it was a cold world for others like Shirley—and for most of those who've chosen to tell their stories here.

∽ ⊚ ⌒

FROM HOME TO THE ORPHANAGE

SHIRLEY CARTER'S STORY begins with alcoholism and sickness, more than eighty years after Anglican minister Robert Fitzgerald Uniacke founded the privately run institution that would go on to shape the lives of generations of children whose parents were dead or addicted, or who were too sick or too poor to take care of them.

Shirley's father was a drinker and a gambler. Her mother contracted tuberculosis and had to go into a sanitarium, so in 1942, her aunt Eileen dropped Shirley, her brother Arthur, and her sister Eileen off at the Veith Street building, where her aunt looked into the baby's big blue eyes and let go of her hand.

The building still stands in the north-end neighbourhood. Remnants of the past still cling to its walls and halls, where former residents now often return and remember, passing closets with peeling Raggedy Ann wallpaper and rickety wooden lockers; passing aged bathroom sinks and almost-one hundred-year-old pipes tucked away in the basement where ghosts are said to whisper.

Shirley has ghosts of her own, and they burn as hot as the leather straps on her bare bum, as tight as the corset-like restraints around her waist, a bedtime ritual that still makes her claustrophobic.

"[It was] a waist-jacket or something....A little undergarment thing that fastened at the back," she says, describing the apparatus, which included long ties that matrons attached to bedrails or mattress springs.

She says one matron tied her and beat her the most. She only remembers her last name. And it's only by her last name—Mrs. Wilkes—that she is listed as a matron in the orphanage's 1946–47 annual report, one of the few remaining annual reports from the 1940s.

Shirley spent many nights unable to move, unable to go to the bathroom, unable to sleep.

"You just want to get free," she remembers. "You feel trapped." Her voice shakes in the telling. "I don't like anybody touching me or grabbing me now—like, holding me—because I feel like I would explode, like I can't get released.

"I wanted to get released," she says. "I didn't want to go to bed. We used to go to bed six-thirty at night—broad daylight—looking at the ceiling, looking out, nothing to do."

At that time, the orphanage had a black cat. It used to jump on Shirley while she was tied to her bed. She was terrified. She still is. She can't be near cats and won't visit anyone who has them, unless they are kept in a separate room.

One night, while she was tied to her bed, what turned out to be a small fire broke out in a cloakroom downstairs on the main floor. Matrons evacuated the other children, but forgot about Shirley and her sister.

Her voice cracks and her words tumble out, rapid and frenetic as she goes back to the moments she thought she'd die.

"I was old enough to think that I may have to lose my life to save all these other kids....My sister Eileen was crying, both of us were crying. I was tied; my sister wasn't tied. Everybody was gone but her and I."

Her sister scrambled to untie the knots and Shirley's panic rose like the smoke below.

I'm going to be burnt, she thought.

"You go, you go," she told her sister. They both eventually escaped.

"It was a rough night," she says now, stopping for an extra breath. "I can't go any further with it....

"I don't like the smell of smoke at all. If I smell smoke...it seems to stay there and I can't get rid of it."

Other smells also linger, triggering memories that make Shirley catch her breath and make her feel like she can't get enough air. On this day in 2016, she keeps a fan close to her face as she recounts other punishments from the matrons who'd later smile for staged pictures when newspaper photographers, dignitaries, or the Ladies' Committee—a group of private citizens that oversaw the facility—came to visit.

The children dressed in fancier clothes for those occasions, and matrons gave them toys that were otherwise stored in a room that was off limits.

But most days were not like that.

Shirley says matrons gave her the strap or locked her in closets—broom closets, vegetable closets, cloak closets—for things as innocent as chewing gum or squabbling with other children.

"I liked to stick up for myself, and if anybody was being hurt I'm going to stand up for them—and I got in a lot of trouble over that," she remembers. "Like, we'd be in line for dinner, for instance, and someone would push me or say something, and I would push back and I'd be caught. I was always being caught, and I spent so many hours in closets that I can't breathe most of the time without [extra] air.

"The downstairs...vegetable closet, they had bushels of vegetables. One time it got so bad I turned them all over. I had to put them all back in, of course. They didn't lock the doors, but you didn't dare open them. And it was dark. You'd come out and you couldn't see....My eyes had to [adjust] to the light for a while. And the upstairs one was the mop closet. So these closets, I've lived in these closets—hours, for hours, until they decided to open it and let me out."

Sometimes she'd scream.

"If you holler any more you're going to stay in there longer," the matrons would say.

Sometimes she'd stay silent.

If I'm real quiet they'll come and let me out, she thought.

The smell of anything musty still makes Shirley feel sick. "I felt like if I don't get some fresh air, I'm going to die.

"I have claustrophobia so bad. I can never get enough air. I don't like doors closed. I don't like anybody up real close in my face. I feel like I've got to push you away, like step back a bit...I feel like it's coming and I can't breathe. I'll have air conditioning on, but I'll have a fan running right beside me on my face so I can breathe, that's how bad...it affected me."

One of her worst memories is a night in a downstairs cloak closet.

She's relived it many times in her mind.

She was on her way to the bathroom. The doorbell rang. She got scared, thinking, *Oh my God, I'm going to get blamed.* She tried running back to the girls' dorm, but the matrons—she's not sure who—caught her and put her in the closet.

She screamed, "Let me out! Let me out!"

Then she heard voices. One of the women said there was a mouse.

Oh my God, where is it? she remembers thinking. *It's pitch dark; I don't know where it is. Is something going to crawl on me?*

All these years later, Shirley isn't sure if there actually was a mouse in there with her or if the matrons were just trying to scare her. If they were, it worked.

"I [thought], 'What am I going to do? I can't stay in here.' I started to get panicky. 'Oh my God, I've got to get out of here!' I said, 'Let me out! Let me out!' and I started kicking the door....I got so terrified that I'm kicking the door down and she said quietly, 'You will spend the night here if I hear one more word out of you.'"

So Shirley stayed quiet as her mind raced.

She's not sure how long she stayed there. She knew the door wasn't locked, but she was too afraid to open it.

I've got to climb out of here somehow, she thought, looking around in the dark, spotting a rack for coats and boots, and above it, a ceiling latch–perhaps a skylight.

I wonder if that would open? she thought. "Then I could get out."

"I didn't know where it led; it took me a long time, but I did it. When I got out, I was outside and I didn't know what to do." Dressed only in her pajamas, Shirley went to the front door and rang the bell.

"I was beat a lot that night. I never forgot it. And I didn't care; I didn't care that night, because I was so relieved to be in my bed and I was no longer afraid....I think you get immune to [the punishments], but the thought of a mouse running on me was [worse]."

Back then, she also punished herself with her own thoughts– chastised herself for feeling the fear that the women who ran the place instilled in her and the other children.

"I thought, 'I shouldn't be like this. I shouldn't be so afraid.' And I used to talk to myself when I was in the closets, the dark. 'I shouldn't be afraid of this thing that I don't even see....

There's probably nothing there.'

"But then I'd think, 'Oh my gosh, the thing might come up behind me.' So I did that, so that was a thing that I shouldn't have done."

A matron strapped Shirley repeatedly that night. She can't say for sure it was Mrs. Wilkes, although she says that matron did most of the beatings and most of the strappings when she was there.

The belt, she says, was Mrs. Wilkes's favourite weapon. And she used it often—so often that Shirley's bum "was sore most of the time."

"We were like good as gold, other than just everyday fights like you would with a sister. They would tell you go up and wait in your bed and come up with a leather strap. They never got you anywhere but the butt, the bottom end, and you would have to wait for your punishment. That was even worse, sitting and waiting for them to come up.

"It takes a lot to get me to cry, because I practiced not [crying]....They would do it until they could get you to cry, and I was determined that I wasn't going to....One time I put a pillow there....I don't know what age I was, but I thought, 'I don't want this again,' and I put a pillow there, and she ripped the pillow out and gave me twice as much."

Shirley tried to fight back in other ways. Once, when Mrs. Wilkes tried to rip gum out of her mouth, Shirley bit her.

"I had gum and you're not allowed to chew gum...and she goes, 'Are you chewing gum?' I was so scared, I had to lie and I said, 'No, Mrs. Wilkes.'

"'You don't have gum?' And I didn't say it again because I was scared, and so she put her hand right in my mouth to take the gum out and I bit her—and paid for that. She really gave me quite a lickin'...."

"It was always straps. 'Go up and I'll be up after to strap you.' It's like torture."

Shirley still wonders what motivated the matron she remembers as "an old lady," with black hair and streaks of grey. "You know, I don't recall her face because it scared me so much, like a witch. Greyish, black hair or something and to me, she was scary. She was scary."

Because the matron's first name doesn't appear in official records, she couldn't be located. It's not clear if she is alive or dead.

In this image, taken inside the orphanage, Shirley Carter is shown second from the left in the back row, with a bow in her hair. *(Shirley Carter)*

∽◦∾

HAPPY MOMENTS, EASILY ERASED

LIKE OTHER FORMER residents through the decades, Shirley's fear was tinged with longing; her pain is almost as much about what didn't happen as it is about the relentless corporal punishment and emotional deprivation she faced year after year after year. It's about the books they never let her read and the toys they never let her touch and the kind words she never heard.

And the happy moments, so easily erased—like wearing a little grey coat and holding a little grey purse, and the "nice people" who gave them to her. They were presents from prospective adoptive parents—one of the childless couples who would often show up to "try out" the children, as another former resident puts it, and who would sometimes send them back.

The Halifax couple took Shirley and her older sister Eileen— who had an intellectual disability because she'd been deprived of oxygen at birth—shopping, and then to their home.

"They bought me a little grey coat with burgundy velvet around the collar, a little hat, a pair of gloves, and a purse to match that coat, and I was so proud and feeling pretty," she remembers. "I don't know how old I was then. I remember it, so I had to be over five....

"So they said, 'Would you like to come and live here?' I said, 'Oh no...we can't; we have to go home [to the orphanage]. We have to go, our brother's home.' And they were very nice; they didn't get mad or anything, and I said, 'You can take the clothes back. It's okay; we can't stay.' And she said, 'No, dear, you can keep those.'

But when they got back to the orphanage, the matrons took the clothes away. Shirley cried.

That's so mean, she remembers thinking. *I can't believe they just did that.*

"I think it was because we didn't want to go."

Many years later, her mother—whom Shirley doesn't remember ever visiting the orphanage—told her a wealthy doctor and his wife had wanted to adopt them, but her mother wouldn't agree to it.

Shirley wonders what her life might have been like if that adoption had happened.

Or if she had lived in a place like the ones she created in her mind, in the orphanage yard, where she'd place stones around the gazebo and pretend they were rooms.

"I was happy doing that," she says on another day in 2018, feeling a little better this time, relieved to unburden herself of memories that have tortured her for so long. "We were playing house....I used to say, 'Okay, this door is going to be the opening and you're going to go in the nice living room' and pretend there was this nice furniture.

"'Look at this nice bed here.'

"We used our imaginations."

A CONFUSING CONCEPT

FINALLY, THE DAY came when Shirley moved to an actual home. Seemingly out of the blue, her father came to the orphanage to get her. They rode on a streetcar and she felt like raising her arms in the air with joy.

"I was happy," she says. "I liked the freedom....I didn't have to worry about being beat."

But home was a confusing concept.

"I was kind of lost," she says.

By now, her family lived in Manning Pool—military housing in Halifax, close to the institution where she had spent nine years (she believes she was the child who lived there the longest). The orphanage beckoned. She felt the need to go back, to visit the only home she had ever known.

When Shirley was around twelve, she started going back to the orphanage for visits, and she did things she hadn't been allowed to do before.

As a child, she'd longed to go inside a locked room full of books, stored behind what she remembers as wire. Only children who were twelve could go inside then, so she'd missed her chance by about a year. But now, on her visits, it was open, and she walked inside and she read to the children who still lived in the place its founders, in their 1859 annual report, had called "a peaceful and happy home."

It seemed different somehow. More peaceful. Happier. The orphanage children seemed to be able to move around more freely, she says, and it was important to her to know they weren't being abused.

Decades later, some children from that time period—the mid-1950s—would remember life there differently: the restraints, the strappings, the beatings with paddles, they say, continued.

As time passed, Shirley's life at home with her parents and her siblings—more siblings—changed.

They had moved to different military barracks near Chebucto Road and she missed the freedom she'd had at Manning Pool, where she had been able to visit the orphanage and wander as she wished. She had loved walking to the Moirs chocolate factory in downtown Halifax, where her aunt Eileen— the woman who'd taken her to the orphanage, the woman who'd visited every month, the woman she'd thought of as a second mother—worked "in a little shop at the front, selling broken bits and cakes."

Shirley would take the broken sweets and day-old bread back home, where her aunt also made sure they all had birthday cakes—something she'd missed in the orphanage.

But on Chebucto Road, the family lived in a tarpaper house that wasn't finished. And Shirley felt trapped again.

"The walls didn't go to the ceiling; they were, like, partly up," she remembers. "There was, like, a little living room with a wood stove, a kitchen; the bedroom was off the living room... and then there was a huge room in the back that all of us kids could fit in."

Her mother and father had had more kids while she and her siblings were in the orphanage. Her sister Marguerite, an infant when they went in, had stayed with their grandmother and their aunt Eileen. Marguerite was home now, too, as were her new siblings—her brother Blair and her sister Marlene, and another boy, Gary, born shortly after Shirley came home.

She didn't blame her parents then, and she doesn't blame them now, for placing her in the orphanage, or for what happened to her inside, even though her mother blamed herself.

"After she heard about me being tied to the bed and stuff she said, 'That really bothered me.'

"My mother was a good woman. I don't want you to think otherwise. I never heard a swear word out of her. She never drank any alcohol. She never smoked. She looked after us kids when we were out the best she could....

"I got a picture printed out on a paper and she was so skinny; she was near death's door when she went into the TB hospital. She had me,...just a new baby, and she was just drained. And I looked at it and said, 'Oh my gosh, what a sin.' No human being should be like that.

"And my mom used to try to say sometimes, 'Shirley, I'm really sorry,' and I said, 'Mom, don't worry about it.'"

Her father was "a good person" too. But he had an addiction that helped shape his children's lives.

"I loved my dad....He was a victim of his alcoholism," she says. "I remember he would just sit there, and he never hollered....He took me to the store to buy tobacco and Zig Zag papers to smoke, and Mom said I was always his favourite.... I didn't really see him drinking. I just heard that he was an alcoholic, he used to go to the taverns."

The family continued to struggle, and Shirley's life changed again.

She loved school. She always had, even back in her orphanage days when she'd longed to read the books locked behind the wire mesh, just beyond her grasp.

Now Shirley was an honours student, but as she was about to go into grade eight, her parents made her quit school so she could help them financially.

She cried, but she did her part.

"I just did what I was supposed to do," she says. "When you're in an orphanage, you do what you're told, and so I thought, 'There's nothing I can do about this, okay? They need to eat.'"

She got jobs at a shoe store and at a department store. She helped her mother with the younger children, and they carried on.

And then her father left. One of her uncles took him to Toronto for work and "he never came back."

As time went on, Shirley wanted to leave too—to fulfill a dream she'd had for as long as she could remember—and one she saw slipping away.

"I left Halifax because I was being burdened by everybody and I didn't have a life. I wanted to be a nurse, and I could see it wasn't going to happen because I had to help people all the time. I said, 'Let me go to Toronto, and I'll send some money home.'"

᠅

A NEW LIFE

SHIRLEY WENT TO Toronto when she was seventeen. She kept her promise until the day her mother died, sending money home even when she was barely making enough to support herself.

She couldn't get into college when she first arrived because she had only finished grade seven, but she took a practical nursing course and got a job. Then she met a man; she became pregnant and had her first child when she was eighteen.

"I didn't want to abandon my job. I went and did housework and scrubbed floors," she remembers.

The family she worked for felt like "a mother and a father." They drove her to the hospital when she went into labour, but she had her baby "alone." They wanted to adopt her daughter, but Shirley wanted to keep her. Children's Aid came to the hospital and arranged for foster parents to take her daughter until Shirley could get back on her feet. She visited her there.

Eventually, she got a job as a nurse's aid at a local hospital, got her daughter back, and raised her child by herself. The father, she says, didn't want to be involved, and she never saw him again.

"I thought, 'I'm strong enough; I can do this myself. What I've been through, I can do this too.' So I went to St. Joseph's Hospital and the nuns were running it. It's a big general hospital; it's got seven floors...and I said to the lady, 'I need a job today; I've got a little baby.'

"They hired me on the spot, and I worked at that hospital for twenty-eight years."

She got married and had other children, but eventually got divorced.

It would be over twenty more years before her professional dream—something she was "born to do"—came true, and before she would become happily married to her second husband, Ed.

She was still working at St. Joseph's and was pregnant with her third daughter, Michele, in 1962, when the past—and more pain—intervened again.

"It's an unusual story," she says. Yet in many ways it's the same—the same story of alcoholism, poverty, and desolation that sent hundreds of children like Shirley to the orphanage over the years.

She was walking down the street in Toronto when she saw a man who looked familiar. "He's walking right towards me, and I said, 'That's my father.' So I go up to this guy when I'm closer and I say, 'Is your name Arthur Lorette?' and he goes, 'Yes.'"

And she said, "Well, I'm your daughter Shirley.

"He gave me a big hug; he was so happy to see me."

Shirley saw him several times at her home; they talked, although about what, she isn't sure. But she says it always felt good.

"He was maybe a proud man, I don't know. He never said he needed anything...and I didn't want to go there." Still, she told him if he ever needed her for anything, to call St. Joseph's and she would come. About two months later, someone from another hospital called. They said Arthur was dying of lung cancer and Shirley should come quickly.

By the time she got there, he was dead.

They gave her an envelope with all of his belongings—just a key and his army service card in a white envelope.

"I just felt so sad that this was a man's life."

Shirley found out where he had lived, and she walked the dark staircase to his room in a seedy area of the city. She could barely see though her tears. "When I opened the door, there was a cot there....It was just a cot. He had nothing, and if I had known, I would have helped him."

Instead, she buried him, in a stranger's suit provided by the funeral home. The army paid, but his military service—she doesn't know what he did or if he was a war veteran—is one more mystery about the man she calls her "hero" for taking her out of the orphanage.

"It was meant to be," she says of their final encounters. "Sometimes life takes you where you have to be."

It eventually took her—or she took herself—to where she was always meant to be. To a profession of care and compassion—something she was so often denied as a child. Something, she says again, she was "born to do."

౿ఌ◉ಌ౿

HELPING OTHERS

SHIRLEY FINALLY BECAME a nurse when she was in her forties. And like so many things in her life, the accomplishment was borne of struggle and grit and perseverance. She went to her local library and found the right books. She studied on

Shirley Carter proudly graduated from nursing school when she was in her forties. *(Shirley Carter)*

her own between shifts. She took a qualifying exam and she got into college as a mature student, and when she graduated she spoke as the valedictorian of her class.

Eventually she practiced for eight years as a nurse in a psychiatric ward for elderly patients—often telling them, "You can rise above all this. You can have a bad life and end up on top....I've been there. You can rise above all that, no matter what happens."

Before that, for twenty-eight years, as a registered nursing assistant, Shirley helped people in other ways. She walked patients and she washed them; she changed their bedpans and she soothed them.

She worked extra hours. She never left early. She loved fulfilling her lifelong need "to look after people."

"I wouldn't care if missed a break. I looked after my patients. I tried to go to see them before they would ring. I never left a shift without checking my patients."

She remembers one young woman in her twenties who was bedridden, dying of ovarian cancer.

"She was in a private room way down at the end of the hall and she rang a lot, and one day an RN was at the desk and she said, 'If she rings one more time....' And I said, 'Hey, wait a minute....She is around your age and she's dying, and she's all by herself down there. All you have to do is go down and comfort her.' And I said, 'If I hear you with that attitude again, I will report you.'...So, I defended these patients."

So did the nuns who ran the hospital. She'd watch them comforting the men and women in their care, sitting with them at night in their rooms.

"I loved them," she says of the nuns. "And they loved me."

She had met other nuns during a brief interlude of kindness amid the turmoil of another time when she too–for different reasons–had been confined to her bed, tied there for hours on end.

The nuns are just one more memory from a past that persists. It's 1945. The Magazine Hill ammunition depot explodes, shattering glass across the city.

Shirley is inside the orphanage and the windows are breaking.

"Put your head down everybody," the matrons scream. "Don't go near the windows!"

"All the glass was falling everywhere," she remembers. "And we were scared." But then terror turned to kindness for scattered moments in a mysterious place. She isn't sure where the orphanage children had gone, but she wasn't scared anymore. It felt like a dream. Or like heaven.

"I thought, 'Am I dead or what?' Shirley remembers. "These [nuns] were so nice, telling us, 'Dear, don't worry; everything's okay.' We were never treated like that."

She still wonders why.

Why the matrons did what they did.

Why the Ladies' Committee, or social workers, or the Province didn't stop them.

Why the provincial government won't apologize for what she considers the negligence of its counterparts in the past.

"I don't remember anybody coming and asking me am I okay," she says, echoing an almost-universal statement from former residents.

"I think it's an atrocity. Nobody bothered—'Too bad; okay'— *stamp*. They go on with their life.

"It's gone now and it's closed—who cares? But that was all my formative years....

"I'm scarred. I'm scarred. Why should I have to live my life like that because of what somebody else did?"

THE PSYCHOLOGICAL EFFECT OF ABUSE

Science has increasingly caught up to what former residents like Shirley Carter innately know: childhood trauma often lasts forever.

A massive study, including seventeen thousand people, from 1995 to 1997, has been a key factor in this awakening, showing how profoundly childhood physical, sexual, and emotional abuse—or neglect, or factors like witnessing domestic violence, or mental illness, or substance abuse in the home, even the separation of parents—can affect people later in life.

It's known as the ACE study—short for the CDC-Kaiser Permanente Adverse Childhood Experiences

(ACE) study—which, according to its researchers, is one of the largest investigations on the subject.

The participants, who are still being monitored today, answered confidential surveys about their childhoods and their health later in life. Researchers found, as outlined in their report, that "almost two thirds of study participants reported at least one ACE" and "more than one in five" recounted three or more adverse childhood experiences. They found exposure to abuse or neglect or other traumatic childhood experiences places children at higher risk for a range of troubles as adults—depression, substance abuse, mental illness, and more.

An accumulation of these experiences increases the risk even further.

Other researchers have since expanded on this work, including Toronto psychiatrist Dr. Robert Maunder, who is deputy-psychiatrist-in-chief and head of research in the department of psychiatry at Mount Sinai Hospital in Toronto. He has seen the effects of childhood trauma up close—not only its links to depression and anxiety, but also to heart disease and bowel disorders and chronic pain and other physical conditions, like fibromyalgia and non-cardiac chest pain, that are not as well understood.

But the kinds of adversity orphanage children faced, and the cumulative effects over time, "kind of leave that ACE scale behind," he says in an interview.

"I mean, you'd have to be remarkably resilient, or [have gone from] that institutional environment to something that was far more supportive and nurturing, to be able to get through that without having a lot of effect later in life."

Many of the former residents have shown tremendous resilience, going on to successful careers. But it's often a struggle in the aftermath.

One kind person in their past—perhaps like Mrs. Fraser, the beloved cook in the orphanage who many residents mention—or some other kind of more-caring oasis amid the turmoil, can help children—and later, adults—cope, says Dr. Maunder, who is also a professor in the University of Toronto's Department of Psychiatry, and co-author, with Dr. Jon Hunter, of *Love, Fear & Health: How Our Attachments to Others Shape Health and Health Care.*

But, he says, "We know way less about resilience than we know about what makes people sick.

"If you look at adults who have a single trauma, even a wartime experience,...a traffic accident, they're a victim of a crime—whatever—from a single trauma, by far the most common outcome is complete recovery. Ninety percent of people are resilient to that type of trauma, which wouldn't be the case for the kind of extensive, accumulated trauma that people growing up in the orphanage...would have.

"There, it would be more exceptional for somebody to have a really resilient outcome."

Subsequent relationships, loving relationships, can make a "tremendous difference," he says.

Some people are just more resilient from the start. Others find comfort where they can.

"If somebody found that their years in that orphanage were the best years in their childhood, then I guess that gives them something to kind of cling to or return to," says Dr. Maunder. "Sometimes there are other relationships which are other mitigating factors, even at the time of the trauma, that can allow some people to be more resilient."

But what researchers do know "for sure" is that childhood trauma increases the risk for later mental illness and chronic physical illnesses like heart disease and stroke.

"The American Heart Association actually put out a scientific statement [in 2018] to make it clear that they're convinced by the evidence that early childhood adversity contributes to cardiovascular disease," he says.

Nobody is sure exactly why. But he says it's likely a combination of physiology—since trauma and major stress can hurt the body's regulatory systems—and lifestyle. Behaviours like smoking or drinking or overeating can play a role.

Even the brain itself can change with trauma, leading people "to learn things that are hard to unlearn," says Dr. Maunder.

Beyond that, on a more basic level, is the emotional pain those who've endured the abuse continue to feel. And as much as researchers and others have learned about the effects of trauma since the orphanage closed, Dr. Maunder says we still have so far to go.

ACE statistics consistently show that 50–60 percent of people have at least one of the ten adverse childhood experiences included in the study, and Dr. Maunder says child abuse is still far too common, as is spanking, which many incorrectly downgrade as an effective parental tool to correct behavior. Spanking is protected under the Canadian Criminal Code, which allows parents and teachers to use so-called reasonable force to discipline children—something he and others have unsuccessfully tried to change.

When we spoke, Dr. Maunder had recently co-written an article for the *Toronto Star* in support of a private members bill—one of many on the subject over the years—to remove the exemption, but he expected the move to fail, as had all the others in the past.

"We are...now at the point in history where we as a medical profession, or as a society, were with respect to smoking in the 1960s," he says. "We have tons of data; we know perfectly well what the problem is, and it takes a couple of decades to change the culture. And without the stories, and without it continuing to be front and centre—

[despite] how important it is and how common it is—you never change the culture....

"The evidence is that physical harm to children increases...their health risks and other risks through life. There is no minimum level that is safe. On the other hand, the evidence that it is useful for improving behavior is zero."

As for the past, Dr. Maunder laments the fact so many children had to face the kinds of physical and emotional harm they did at the orphanage, or at home, or in their foster homes.

"I just kind of waver back and forth, I suppose, from being heartbroken and being enraged," he says. "The rage is useful because it fuels advocacy, but mostly it just makes you want to cry. It makes you want to go home and hug your kids."

Chapter Two:
Heartbreak Songs
Linda Gray-LeBlanc

A TEAR ROLLS DOWN LINDA Gray-LeBlanc's cheek and stops, frozen in place, like memories from sixty years ago.

She wipes it away, but another appears.

In the dorm room, where matrons tied her to her bed, or hit her with paddles.

In "the horror room," where she slept on cots and peed in bedpans.

By the fence, where her father visited—once—and gave her an orange.

"You just want to cry all the time," says Linda, standing where she once slept. "You just can't get rid of it. You just can't get rid of it."

It's noon in late July 2017. Sunlight dapples old checkered floors, brightens children's bumble bee stickers—"bee happy"—and intensifies her tears, stains from the past.

On this day, inside Veith House, the former girls' dorm is a preschool, with pretend kitchens and ironing boards, washers and dryers, and rainbow colours that glow in the sun.

As a child, Linda spent many terrifying days and nights here. As a senior citizen, in her late sixties, she sometimes comes back, giving tours to history buffs or former residents— in a place where children now play, where social workers meet, and community groups gather.

But the past shadows everything.

It always has.

From her earliest memories to today, as she walks up creaking wooden steps, down dark narrow hallways, past old corners where she used to stand all night long.

⤳ ◎ ⤳

A PLACE OF SQUALOR

BEFORE THE ORPHANAGE, Linda lived in a cramped flat with fourteen siblings and her alcoholic parents.

It was a place of beatings and squalor and hunger.

"They got into the booze, both of them," she recalled when we spoke a few years earlier, sitting in her Halifax apartment, rain dripping down her windows, tears falling down her face, thinking about what led her to the orphanage's door.

"They were both alcoholics, that's why we were taken away from them," she says.

"We were living in Halifax at that time, Water Street....I think it was a two-bedroom flat and it was full of bedbugs and cockroaches and mice...and that's where a lot of my fears came of mice, crawling creatures, and of the dark. I still have it today, all those things. I sleep with a light on, or my TV on."

The people in her life were just as frightening. Memories of them, and the strangers she met later, plague her body and her mind. She's been diagnosed with post-traumatic stress disorder. She's been on anti-depressants and anti-anxiety medication for years.

She's tried to end her own life.

"I remember the fighting," Linda says of her early life. "Dad was a very, very calm and quiet man and Mom was just totally opposite. She had a very mean streak into her....I can remember Dad coming home drunk and Mom chasing him down the stairs and throwing knives at him....

"Dad was never home. He was always out either drinking or working...but Mom....If we weren't in the house at a certain time, she'd be standing behind the door waiting with a stick and she used to paddle us anywhere. "

When they weren't home, she and her siblings used to "roam the streets"–missing school, sharing shoes, searching for food.

She was just six when she'd sneak into a downtown factory to steal bananas and steal from trucks.

"We were always hungry," she remembers. "We had no food, hardly ever....The pop trucks, they used to have the sliding doors, so when the guy was on one side of the truck loading, I'd be on the other side of the truck to help myself to a pop....

"We were hungry, and the pop filled your stomach....I really don't remember a meal. Hunger, I think your stomach gets used to hunger....You go to bed hungry."

In those days there were always new hungry mouths to feed. Three of the babies died in infancy. Her mother always blamed Linda's oldest sister, Marilyn, for one of the deaths. She told her she'd rolled over on her baby sister in bed and had smothered her. That was a lie. Linda saw the baby's death certificate decades later; she had died of pneumonia and malnutrition.

As much as she remembers her mother's cruelty, she recalls these and other infants at her mother's breast.

"She'd pull out her breast and she'd say, 'Here, you want some?' she remembers, thinking too about how she slept in a dresser drawer and how Marilyn, three years older, was more like a mother.

"She changed the baby's diapers and there was maggots crawling all over the baby's bum. So Mom never looked

Linda Gray-LeBlanc, just seven years old in 1957, stands in the yard of the Halifax Protestant Orphanage. (*Linda Gray-LeBlanc*)

after us; that's how she was. She was just drunk; my brother used to say when Dad would come in the door, Mom would be pushing a man out the window. She always had men. I mean, Dad knew about it; there was always men."

One man, she doesn't know his name, sexually molested Linda in her parents' home when she was about six, something that would happen to her again years later.

જ⊚જ

THE HORROR ROOM

LINDA ENTERED THE Protestant Orphans' Home when she was seven, in 1957, the year a judge asked her if she'd rather go to the orphanage or stay home. She chose the orphanage.

The "horror room" is her first memory there. Its real name was the isolation room.

For decades, newly admitted children were forced to stay there for two weeks to make sure they didn't spread lice or diseases to the other occupants.

For children already frightened by their past experiences, or by the recent deaths of their parents, or after having been abandoned by their parents, this was an especially scary introduction to their new home.

Linda and four of her siblings—Bev, Wendy, Debbie, and Carol—went there after their mother left and their father tried to raise them on his own. He eventually called Children's Aid. Marilyn joined them a few months later. The others went to different institutions or into foster care.

"We were put in this room and the door was locked," Linda says of the area she still rushes past or leaves quickly when visiting Veith House today. "The five of us were put in there, the door was locked, and we ate and slept and peed and fought and cried in that room for two weeks."

It was pitch dark at night, she says, and she felt trapped during the day.

She stands there on a summer day, looking in but staying close to the door.

"It is small. Can you see five kids in here?" she says, her eyes watering once more. "[You feel] caught, just caught....You're taken from your parents, go through that door and you're put in prison and you're locked away....

"The kids that come through now, they still remember this was 'the horror room.' We had one gentleman come last year or the year before....He walked in through the door and just looked at this room and fell on the floor crying."

Linda has cried many tears over it, too. Some of her phobias started in the tiny room, which was later used as an office, and is now almost bare except for coffee, tea, a few cups, and a table and chairs.

"I've got to have a clear window. I can't have my doors closed," she says. "Never....If I go into the hospital, they can't pull that curtain around me, because I start panicking."

But when she and her siblings left the isolation room, new horrors began.

⸙

NEW HORRORS

"THE DAY WE were taken out of isolation, it was lunchtime and they marched us down the fire escape—you were never allowed to use the stairs there, it was always the fire escape. So we marched down the fire escape into the lunch room, and we walk in and there's twenty to thirty kids sitting there, and all you could feel was all these eyes upon you....Everybody just looking at you."

Linda's phobias followed her to the girls' dormitory, where, for the next year, matrons regularly tied her to her bed, using the same type of restraints they had used on Shirley Carter a decade earlier.

"At night if you misbehaved and you couldn't settle down, you were given a bedjacket. You're tied in bed. A straightjacket, that's what it was....If you wet the bed, you were given a lickin' or forced to stand in a corner."

She didn't wet the bed. But her sister Bev often did, and the matrons beat her with wooden paddles that looked like Ping-Pong paddles.

Sometimes they were able to hide the wet sheets.

"[Bev] would crawl under the beds and she would change her clothes and throw them in the wash, and she'd sleep with me. Then we'd wake up early in the morning before anybody got up and we'd change her bed."

But sometimes they couldn't.

"I must have been a bad little bugger," she says with a grim laugh, "because I used to be in that bedjacket all the time."

She'd lie there staring at the ceiling, sucking her thumb, twirling her hair with her finger. She twirls it again, standing in the dorm sixty years later. "Even today, when I'm lying in bed...I'm still playing with my hair. It's soothing. It relaxes you," she says.

She stops now and looks around, walks through the door and stands in a corner. Children's handprints, in paints of yellow and brown and red, hang on a poster above.

"If you didn't stay in bed,...you stood in the corner," she says. "I remember waking up one night after standing in this corner, in the bathroom sitting on the toilet, and I said, 'Oh my God, I'm not supposed to be here; if she comes and catches me I'm going to be punished again.' So I come back and I stood back in the corner and I stood there all night long. [The matron] just left me standing there."

If she got caught, she knew she'd get the paddle—punishment for everything from "carrying on with other kids" to laughing. "Stupid things, you know. Being a child."

As a child Linda liked knowing that then–head matron Sara Patriquin—who records indicate was in charge from the late 1940s until the late 1950s—was close by. Her bedroom was right across the hall from the girls' dorm. Like other former residents from the 1950s, Linda speaks of Patriquin fondly—uses words like "nice" and "kind."

But she pauses now, by the corner, and wonders.

"I never remember her punishing me, but she had to know all this stuff was going on. She had to. And for me to be standing in that corner and her door always open, she had to be going along with the matrons."

But the thought drifts away. She remembers how Patriquin comforted her when she cried, how she let her into her room and curled her hair, how she saved her life one night in the girls' bathroom a few steps away.

She looks to where it happened. Three of the original bathroom sinks still stand, stained pink or chipped black. The footed bathtubs are hidden behind a long wooden cupboard, but she can still picture them—and she can still feel the panic she felt when her head was under water.

She had been taking a bath.

"This was the side I was in. [The matron] tried to drown me," she says, touching the cupboard, standing on the old linoleum floor. "They had a little soap dish on the side, and I don't know if I wasn't paying attention, or just being dumb, or what, and [the matron] said, 'Put the soap in the dish.' I didn't do it, and she just grabbed me by the back of the neck and just ducked me under," she remembers.

"She was holding me there, and I was kicking and screaming, and Mrs. Patriquin came in and grabbed her. She got me up and said, 'Go to your room and get changed.'

"Of course [I was] crying and gasping for air....[Mrs. Patriquin] walked that woman right out the door. I remember she was gone that night."

She doesn't remember the woman's name, or the names of the other matrons. But she can't forget what they did in the dorm, in the bathroom, in the dining hall.

"That day the matron made me eat the fat off the pork chops....She said, 'Eat the fat on your plate,' and I said, 'I can't eat the fat.' She said, 'Eat it.'

"I ate it, and then all of a sudden I just threw it up all over her, and of course I got beaten for it.

"One kid told me he ate his, threw up in his plate, and she made him eat it."

Residents from other decades also describe a similarly strict dinnertime ritual. Matrons forced children to finish everything on their plates, whether they liked it or not, before allowing them to leave the table. Sometimes they'd sit there for hours, or all night long.

They treated them differently when the Ladies' Committee, who oversaw the orphanage, visited. Staff usually knew when they were coming. The children were dressed in nicer clothes and allowed to hold toys which were otherwise off limits, except on birthdays or Christmas Day, when they'd line up in the large empty playroom, boys on one side, girls on the other, before entering a smaller room with presents and a Christmas tree.

"They'd give gifts—boy, girl, boy, girl," Linda remembers, standing in what's now a community room.

She opens the door to the fire escape—musty, like it was back then—and another memory.

"We were never allowed to use the [main] steps, always had to use the fire escape. That was to keep the noise level down of children running up the stairs."

Linda moves to another room, where parents were allowed to visit. It prompts another memory: her father, who came to visit once, outside, by the fence.

"He come and stood by the fence right here," she says, touching the wire, looking into the yard on the quiet, tree-lined street, past a plaque commemorating the orphanage's previous building, destroyed by the Halifax Explosion.

"He asked us if we liked it here, and of course we said yes. He gave me an orange and he just said, 'Be good,' and he never came back."

She saw him a few more times after that, outside taverns on Gottingen Street. She'd rap on the door. "Can I talk to my daddy?" He'd come out and give her a dime. Those were the last times she saw him.

She went to his funeral in 1962.

But for many years, she had called another man "father."

⤳ ◎ ⤸

THE HAPPIEST TIME

LINDA'S FIRST FOSTER home was in West Jeddore, Nova Scotia; she was there between the ages of eight and nine with two of her sisters. Her other siblings were sent to different foster homes or raised by relatives or placed in care.

"It was the best time I had in my life; it was the happiest time I had in my life because of the neighbours," she says. "The people in the neighbourhood looked after us."

Their strict Baptist foster parents—"just out for the money"—didn't.

They'd hit Linda and her sisters with kindling sticks; Linda herself was "whacked many a time."

They made them sleep outside in tents, even in thunderstorms, all summer long. They made them work

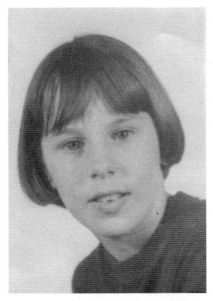

Linda Gray-LeBlanc in 1959, when she went to live at a foster home in West Jeddore, Nova Scotia. (*Linda Gray-LeBlanc*)

all day, feeding the chickens, cleaning the barn.

"We were there to work," she says.

But neighbours sometimes took them in, and they had real friends for the first time in their lives. They went blueberry picking and they played and they swam—even on Sundays, which was forbidden—and her friends dried her hair so her foster parents wouldn't know.

She liked to run—"run and run and run"—through the fields, on the gravel roads, out to the water, where they'd all sail on dinghies, some of them hanging on the sides, out to the flats and another world, where playing cards or swimming on Sundays wasn't a sin.

"In the wintertime in the harbour we used to get these great big icebergs and we'd go hopping on these in...East Jeddore Harbour."

She laughs, thinking about those good times. But they didn't last.

The neighbours, who helped feed them, who were kind to them, eventually told authorities they'd been sleeping outside, that they weren't allowed in the house, that the doors were locked at night. Those memories haunt Linda to this day; she thinks of the thunderstorms that boomed overhead as she and her sisters lay wet in their tent, their clothes damp and musty, their pulses racing—the way hers still races today when the sky cracks anew and she takes her pillow into her bathroom and stays there until it stops.

But her fears worsened after the neighbours—still trying to help—reported the foster parents to social workers. "The Children's Aid just come down one day and said, 'You're moving.'"

Marilyn, thirteen or fourteen at the time, had already left a few months earlier, placed in St. Paul's Home for Girls.

"When she left—oh my God," Linda says, "I thought my world was ending, because she was my mother."

༺༻

A HOSTILE HOME

SOCIAL WORKERS MOVED Linda and Wendy to a foster home in Clam Harbour, and everything got worse. She was eleven and stayed until she was eighteen, but they sent Wendy away soon afterward.

And that's when the sexual abuse began.

At first in the root cellar, where she says her foster father threatened her—told her not to tell, told her no one would believe her. And then in the woods, and then in her bedroom, in an unrelentingly hostile home.

"From that day on, it was every day," she says of the assaults. "I hadn't even started my period yet....He would molest me no matter where I went. I tried to avoid him, but [my foster mother] was not helping. He would say, 'Come on, let's go picking blueberries.'

"'I don't want to go.'"

Her foster mother would say, "Don't you be so lazy, you go with your father."

"I'd have to go in the woods with him and he'd molest me. Then he started coming to my bedroom. Like, he used to get up [at] five o'clock in the morning...and he used to come to my room every morning. I used to roll up in a blanket before I'd hear him coming and he'd come up and he'd pull the blankets off."

It continued until Linda was seventeen.

She cries, thinking about the abuse and the emotional cruelty that was also part of her daily life. She lived in the house with her foster parents, two of their four sons, her foster mother's mom, and various other foster children. But she felt alone.

"She never took to me," she says of her foster mother. "She was so mean; her words were so mean. Like when Wendy and I would be out playing, she'd call Wendy over and say, 'Don't play with her....Your sister is a bad girl.'

"It's a wonder I don't have an eating disorder. I mean, she was a good cook, they fed you....Their meals were always good. I was always the first one at the table, and she used to say every time, 'Well, you might know; you're always the first one at the table. You know when to come for your meals.' And it would hurt me, and I would go upstairs and I wouldn't eat. At times I would not eat for days because of the things she used to say,...

and of course the grandmother was always the same way," says Linda.

"You were always 'that foster kid,' and if you don't behave yourself you were to be put in St. Paul's Home for Girls with your sister because she is bad, or you'll be sent to...[a home] for very bad girls."

But sometimes Linda rebelled. The desperation overwhelmed her and she ran away.

Once, she ran inside the unlocked church "and just sat there and cried all day long."

Once, she got on her bike and pedalled for miles down the highway, hoping to reach her mother in Ontario.

Once, she ran into the woods with a gun, a few days after a rare outing with old friends led to an encounter with her foster father.

"We went down to where he [went] fishing and I asked to go, because I wanted to see a couple of school friends down there," she remembers.

"He said, 'Okay, you can go....Don't be long.'

"We–three of the girls and one boy–we went walking around the shore, just talking, and it felt so good, and before we knew it, the time had flown. So we were walking by, and all of a sudden there he was. He came up and he grabbed me by the hair and he pulled my hair and he was shaking me–this was my foster father–and he said, 'You were supposed to be back here.' He was going on and on...and I kept saying to him, 'We didn't do nothing; we were just walking and talking.' And he was shouting and hollering at me, and it was just on the tip of my tongue to say, 'At least they're not abusing me.' It was just there and I just couldn't get it out.

"And so the next day I was just a nervous wreck....I think I was suicidal. I went...to babysit, and I just sat there crying the whole night after the kids were in bed, and I got on the phone and I called Ontario–I called Marilyn, and I was going to tell her everything...[but] she wasn't home," Linda says.

"The next day, they went to town and left me home by myself, and they had a gun rack; we were never allowed to touch the guns. After they'd gone, I took the .22 and I put the bullets in it and I went into the woods."

Linda stops for a moment, back in her apartment, as the rain falls and her tears flow.

"I don't know what stopped me," she says. "I must have been suicidal. I was a basket case."

She was around thirteen or fourteen.

Social workers visited occasionally. But even when one showed up unexpectedly at her school and asked her questions, Linda didn't tell her what was really happening.

"She must have known something was going on....I can't remember what questions she'd ask, but I just sat there looking at the floor. I didn't trust her. They put me there–why would I trust them?"

And by then she had vowed not to trust anyone or anything again.

She breaks down now, sobbing, as a heartbreaking memory appears.

"She used to take in other foster kids, and she had these two little boys come. They were around two or three years old, Christopher and Wade, and I just fell in love with them two boys. Christopher, he went into a foster home, so then it was just me and Wade, and...I just loved Wade. But [my foster mother] used to be so jealous—I don't know why—of my affections to Wade. He used to cry, and I used to take him in my bed and she would come up and [say], 'Get in your bed.' He'd stand up in his crib and he'd hold his hands out for me to take him, and she'd smack him and make him get down in bed again.

"You know, he was the only thing I cared about, and then they decided that he was going to be adopted. The day the social worker come down to get him, I just cried and begged them to take me with him. I never heard from him again."

She reaches for a tissue and wipes her eyes as the rain streaks her window.

"All my life it's been like that."

After that, she distanced herself from the other foster kids they took in—and from everyone else. "I just turned into such a nervous, lonely kid with him molesting me, her mentally abusing me, the cruel things she was saying...I was just lost....

"I had no friends in the neighbourhood," she says. "Kids didn't want to play with me because I was a foster kid."

Linda wrote about it all decades later in her self-published book, *I Was Called 'That Foster Kid:' The True Story of a Foster Child*, keeping the names of her abusers to herself.

Abuse in the orphanage, she says, was never sexual, but the physical and emotional trauma haunts her still. She thinks it always will.

It contributed to her "breakdown" more than a decade ago; she spent a year in the Nova Scotia Hospital (a psychiatric hospital in Dartmouth, Nova Scotia), where she had multiple shock treatments. She says they've helped, but she hasn't gotten rid of the panic attacks that still make her heart race and her chest tighten, make her fingers tingle, make her feel dizzy.

"I feel like I'm having a heart attack," she says.

And she feels like "that little kid"—again.

꿍Ꙩꙩ

A KINDER MATRON

LINDA FELT LIKE "that little kid" again the first time she walked back inside the orphanage as an adult.

She had just turned eighteen when fate handed her a twist: a chance to work at the place where she had once been so afraid. But after all those years of abuse by her foster father, the orphanage seemed like a refuge. She took the job.

The matrons still ran the facility "like a prison." The kids had regimented times to eat and sleep and be home from school. Bells rang to signal the order of the day.

Children were no longer tied to their beds or locked in closets or forced to stand in corners all night, she says. But they might be put in corners for an hour as a time-out, and they still might be hit with the paddle.

She used the paddle herself a couple of times too.

"That's something I've always regretted," she says. "It was the system; it was what you were supposed to do. It was part of the rules of working in the orphanage."

Linda worked there from 1967 until the facility closed in 1970—the year she turned twenty-one and got married to the man who would become the father of her two sons. Today he is her husband of almost fifty years.

But she says she tried to change the rules when she worked there. On her days off, she took the kids swimming, on bus rides, to movies. At night, she read them stories until they fell asleep.

When she was eighteen, Linda Gray-LeBlanc returned to the Halifax Protestant Orphans' Home as an employee. Here, she stands with some residents in 1968. *(Linda Gray-LeBlanc)*

She left her bedroom door open so she could hear them if they cried, and she played them music, something she had never heard in the dormitory or in the playroom or in the halls as a child.

She stands there now, on a summer day, outside the bedroom where she used to keep an old record player—letting the voices of Hank Williams and Conway Twitty and Kitty Wells (her favourite) drift down through the darkness.

"I used to love her music; I'd sing and the kids would laugh," Linda says, thinking of Wells—a diviner of lost love and "aching hearts," forced to face a "cold and lonely dawn."

She looks down the empty hallway, dark still on a summer's day. And she sighs.

"Heartbreak songs."

Chapter Three:
Better Than Home
Leonard Chater and Joe Gooey

L EONARD AND BILL CHATER WATCHED the lights flicker across the harbour.

And sang themselves to sleep to the beat of blinking letters and the echo of aching hearts.

Sometimes they'd wake there the next morning—on the floor of the strange, otherworldly house near the water, where the brothers had unexpectedly found themselves as children.

But for those moments by the window of the boys' dorm in the orphanage, what seemed like magic and imagination took the boys somewhere else—a place where no one hit them or made them stand in corners. Where no one threw rocks at them from across a fence. Where no one mocked them for being "orphans."

Leonard can still picture that old Dartmouth Esso sign, its giant neon letters glowing red in the distance. And he can feel the comfort it gave him all those years ago.

"E-S-S-O! E-S-S-O!" he and Bill would sing as each of the gas station's letters lit the sky and then beamed like beacons across the night.

It helped soothe the loneliness and the sorrow and the noises in the dark dorm, where they stayed with all the other lonely boys, including a disabled child, tied to his bed, who moaned and rocked himself to sleep.

"The letters would light up red...and then the whole thing would sparkle," Leonard remembers. "And then it would go back to 'Esso' and we'd sit there for hours and we'd just watch this sign reflect on the water....It was hard for us; we missed our previous life....The switch was just turned off and we were moved to another planet."

Leonard's previous life had ended on another night; one of his earliest memories. A night before Christmas, mid-December 1956, when he saw blood and an ambulance—and his mother crawling on the floor.

He was five. They were living in Shannon Park—military housing in Dartmouth, Nova Scotia. His father was in the navy and at sea off the coast of Cuba.

His brother, Bill, his little sister, Grace, and his oldest sister, Anne, were asleep.

"She was very ill," Leonard says of his mother. "She had some condition where her blood vessels inside of her body were weak; they were breaking and she would hemorrhage internally and they couldn't stop the bleeding...."

"I woke up because she was coughing and spitting up blood quite a bit. She got on her hands and knees and...she crawled next door to the neighbours'."

They brought her back to bed and called an ambulance.

Leonard was scared and confused. He thinks, as sick as she was, his mom tried to alleviate his fear.

"I remember her being rolled out to the ambulance, and she put her hand up and she grabbed the ambulance guy's arm to stop, and she looked over at me and we caught eye-to-eye and she smiled.

"And then her arm dropped and they took her out."

That was the last time he saw her. For years he thought she had died that night—December 11, 1956. But he recently learned she had stayed in hospital a few days longer. She died December 15, 1956, from gastric hemorrhaging—essentially, she bled to death internally.

His father flew home and over the next two weeks arranged for her funeral and burial.

"None of us kids were allowed to go to her funeral," Leonard says, "because they thought we were too young and it would be too hard on us." So they stayed with neighbours.

His father, expected

Leonard Chater's mother, Jane. *(Leonard Chater)*

back to sea, asked his mother if she would look after the children full-time in Ontario.

She refused then, but years later she would help raise them—years that are among Leonard's worst memories—worse even than the orphanage, a sentiment echoed by some other former residents, whose lives before or after blur the lines between good and bad.

Leonard, his older brother, Bill, and their little sister, Grace, entered the orphanage around late December 1956 or early January 1957.

His memories are vivid half a century later.

"I don't remember who brought us in, but I remember being scared going in the door and being told this is where we were going to live.

"We knew that mom was sick; we had been told that she had died but I don't think I really knew what death was, because

Leonard Chater is shown here with his siblings and other unidentified children. Leonard, (far left), his older brother, Bill (centre), and their sister, Grace (front, far right), all entered the orphanage in late December 1956 or early January 1957. *(Leonard Chater)*

I had never had anybody else that I knew that had died. So I guess we knew she wasn't coming back—that this was our new life."

But a surreal life, and an unreal life, from the moment he walked through the door.

"It's something like when you watch *The Wizard of Oz*. It's black and white, and when she opens the door, when she lands there, everything's colour and it's like a new awareness; it's probably why I remember it.

"It's a milestone in my life."

His life in the orphanage was strict and structured, but when he looks back, the good always mingles with the bad—prisms of colour in the darkness.

On warm days, he loved going out back, swimming in the wading pool or swinging from a rope on a big tree.

But sometimes neighbourhood kids walked by, outside the wrought-iron fence that separated his life from theirs.

"They'd pick up sticks…and they'd run back and forth with this stick on the wrought-iron fence; it would be clacking back and forth and they'd be yelling at us: 'Orphans, orphans, orphans!' And sometimes they'd throw rocks at us, and sticks. It was pretty traumatic.

"I couldn't understand why they would do this, and sometimes I held onto my big brother when the rocks were coming; I was kind of scared, but I started to realize that we were different than them."

Even when he returns decades later, Leonard still feels the divide.

He thinks of the first time.

"I went along that fence, and the memories were coming back to me on that. It still bothers me, you know,...because I could still sort of hear the kids running by with their sticks, saying, 'Orphan, orphan, orphan!'"

He wasn't an orphan. But Leonard doesn't remember his father ever visiting the place where he'd be swimming or swinging one day and standing in a corner the next.

He doesn't remember why he was punished. But he remembers the pain.

"They used to...make you stand in the corner with your hands up high, and after five minutes your arms would get so heavy they'd start dropping. They'd come in and they'd check on you: 'Get your hands [up]!' and you'd get your hands up, and by the time a half-hour was over, boy, it hurt pretty hard."

Matrons hit him, too—with their hands, he says. They hit his brother with "a piece of wood"—like the paddle other residents describe.

The emotional pain, he thinks, was worse.

His oldest sister—who had a different father, and who lived somewhere else—visited once or twice. She took them to the corner store, where they'd spend the five-cent weekly allowance from their father on shoestring licorice they braided and ate on the way back.

But they missed their mom—who, a priest told them, had become "an angel in heaven." And they missed their dad, a Korean War veteran, who was still out at sea.

And eventually, they missed some of the friends they had made in the place that was now their home.

"Me and my brother, we probably had about four really close friends—guys—there. I remember the one time a young couple came to visit, and they were looking at some of the kids, and one of our good friends...was picked.

"This couple had come and they had talked to him, and they came back at a later date when they came to pick him up to adopt him, and...he was just so happy—his face was—because he was always down before, you know?

"And it was a big thing. I remember hearing kids talking that it was a big thing: someday somebody would come through that door and adopt you and take you out of that place," Leonard says.

"He was so happy, and I remember him hugging me and Bill in the lobby and then him running to his new parents. And he turned, and he waved, and he said 'Bye!' with a big smile on his face—and he was gone.

"And I felt happy that he found somebody—that somebody came and took him out of this place—and then I remember being really down when the door closed, and here I am—still there."

Leonard stayed at the orphanage for almost a year, from ages five to six, hearing the taunts, feeling the loneliness, singing through the nights when the disabled boy, whose skull hadn't properly developed, who wore a helmet to protect his head, lay tied to his bed rocking himself to sleep.

And then, their grandmother came to get them.

"I thought we were going to the same life that we had [before], but little did I know that it was going to be a lot different."

HIS GRANDMOTHER'S FISTS

THE INSIDE OF Leonard's lip still bears the scars from his grandmother's fists. His mind still bears the trauma of her belt lashing his bare skin. He remembers the welts rising on the back of his legs and on his behind.

It was far worse than anything he had faced at the orphanage.

"We had physical beatings–like, really, really bad," he says, calling his grandmother a "bitter" woman, who resented having to take care of Leonard and his siblings.

So she punished them for even minor missteps.

"She was a clean freak and everything had to be spotless, and so we were always in clean clothes, clean face–'wash your hands; brush your teeth'–and I remember one time I got up on the bath and there was a window above the bath and there was steam on the window. I couldn't see, and I cleaned it off so I could see outside, because I think it was snowing or something.

"And then I finished my bath I went to bed, and my grandmother went in and saw these hand prints....She wanted to know who did this, so she brought all of us out, all four of us–my oldest sister, Anne,...[had] resumed living with us–so she had all four of us in the hallway...and she made us all strip in the hallway.

"She wanted to know who did that, and I was so terrified I was afraid to say. So she took a belt and she whipped us with the belt to the point where there was welts standing off the backs of our legs and our bums. They [stuck out] a good eighth of an inch....

"This went on for, like, twenty minutes, and I remember looking at one of my sister's bums, and right from her bum down to her knees it was just stripes, red stripes across. Finally I had to stop it, and I told her it was me—and then I got an additional beating. I remember rubbing my hand down my side, just feeling the welts down my side.

"And this went on quite a bit."

And so did other startling abuse.

"Another thing she would do: if you did something wrong, she would turn to walk away and she'd swing around and—*whack!* Right in the mouth. To this day, my lower lip is bigger than it should be. If you pull it down, it's all scar tissue in behind; you can see the scars. So many times."

So many times—at first in Shannon Park and later, when they moved to a farm near Windsor, Nova Scotia.

Until Leonard, then twelve, couldn't take it anymore.

"I just lost it one day when I was lying naked on the bed and my legs were being strapped with a leather strap, to the point where they were just welted right out. I just lost it, and I reached up and I grabbed the belt from my grandmother, and she went running," Leonard recalls. "She locked herself in her bedroom and she made sure that my dad knew all about this, and I got punished for my behaviour to my grandmother."

Sometimes, when his grandmother became especially violent, Leonard's father intervened.

"He lit into my grandmother quite a few times, to the point where she was in tears and she said, 'Well, you have no idea what it's like in here living with these little bastards.'"

But Leonard's dad could be violent too.

"He would take us out by the barn and he would slap you around to the point where you would get angry to hit back. And then he'd hit you to sort of put you right on your ass. He'd hit you good; he wouldn't spank you, he'd just slap you around until you'd just had enough and you'd start fighting back, and he'd just deck you, and that was it.

"It was a pretty rough upbringing."

A pretty rough upbringing—Leonard believes that's true for many others.

"People from that era were used to hard times," says the former diesel mechanic and retired postal worker who's now a father of three grown daughters, and grandfather of two—a boy and a girl.

And as hard as his childhood was, he figures others had it worse. But sometimes, he can't help but look back on his own. He's researched his family history—"searching for years, trying to get my life together."

And he's returned to the orphanage over and over as the years passed. He's walked past the fence and through the door. He's stepped down the halls and up the stairs.

And he's stood by the window that looks to the water.

And he's closed his eyes.

And he's felt a lump in his throat.

And he's imagined "the letters lighting up at night."

❧ ◉ ☙

JOE GOOEY

JOE GOOEY LIVED in the orphanage at a different time than Leonard Chater and they had different experiences—but their perspectives on the facility are remarkably similar.

Leonard thinks it was a "necessary" institution for kids like him.

Joe had nowhere else to go. And, he says, it was far better than home. He lived at the orphanage, intermittently, from

Joe Gooey at thirteen years of age. *(Joe Gooey)*

1951 to 1955—just a few years before Leonard.

He had a rough upbringing, too—both before he arrived and after he left. He says his early years at the orphanage were also "terrible," but he still sees things through a different lens than most.

The orphanage, he says, was "the best place we ever lived." The food there was better than the hunger at home.

A bed of his own was better than sharing one with his mother, father, and siblings—"three at one end and three at the other."

A strict, sometimes scary, institution was better than a dark, dirty room in the back of a laundry in Truro, where he and his family lived until his father died and his mother, Florence, started drinking more heavily.

"She was always drunk, always drunk," Joe says. "She was the nicest lady before she started drinking, but after she started drinking it was terrible....

"She was an alcoholic....The Children's Aid came around—gave us so much food and stuff, and they said they didn't want to separate us because of our background. We were half Chinese;...my mother was white Canadian, my father was Chinese from Hong Kong."

Joe found records later saying his father, Soo Hoo Kee Gooey, had moved to Truro in 1946 and "operated" Tom's Laundry. It isn't clear if he owned the business, but documents show he didn't own the building, since the family paid twenty-eight dollars a month in rent and was eventually evicted.

After Joe's father died, on January 16, 1951, the family was destitute. His mother had siblings and her parents were still alive, but Joe says they'd disowned her because she had married a Chinese man.

"None of those people would look after us."

The Children's Aid Society of Colchester County intervened shortly before Joe's father died. It was a few days before Christmas 1950, and he was still in Colchester County Hospital. His hospitalization, according to the case history Joe later obtained through a Freedom of Information request—left the family "without adequate means of support."

"The town was giving relief [six dollars per week] plus fuel. It was rumoured Mrs. Gooey was drinking a lot and not giving her children proper care," writes the society's then–executive director. "The Salvation Army and Christian Alliance Mission have both taken an interest in the Gooey family and hence the family were taken care of during the Christmas season. After Mr. Gooey's death on January 16, Mrs. Gooey made application for Mothers Allowance. Mothers Allowance was granted but it has been administered by our Agency."

Mrs. Gooey and her children were living, according to the society's report, in "squalor."

Joe describes it as "dark" and "dirty," and the case history mirrors his memory. "Tom's laundry in which they are living is not fit for family living," it says.

> The rooms are very black, the furniture is not adequate and the only source of heat is a small heater. All the food is cooked or heated on this stove. The case has been known to the Town of Truro since Mr. Gooey's death and everyone has been concerned over the welfare of the children and the behavior of the mother....
>
> The home in which the family have been living is situated on Waddell Street, one of the poorer areas in the Town of Truro. It is a laundry consisting of three rooms, laundry, kitchen and what may be called a bedroom. The walls are black and the whole thing presents a dreary unkempt appearance.

Townspeople tried to find them other living quarters after the family received an eviction notice from the building's owner, but authorities eventually decided the children shouldn't be left with their mother.

"There has been much concern over the ability of Mrs. Gooey to care for her children. Living conditions are unsatisfactory and although Mrs. Gooey is fond of her children and has not mistreated them bodily, it is felt that it would be in the best interest of the children to make them wards of the Children's Aid Society."

Their race appears to have been a factor in what happened next. It's mentioned several times in the case report, dated May 10, 1951.

"The Chinese features are prominent in all four children. They are all attractive, bright, friendly and well-mannered children," it says.

> The Orphanages have been contacted in an effort to place this family since it is workers' opinion that these children should not be placed in country foster homes nor too far from people of their own race. The religious angle has been a difficult one since all four children have been baptized Roman Catholic but have always attended a Protestant Mission. We recommend that the four children be placed together in an institution in the City of Halifax.

Why they ended up in the Protestant orphanage isn't clear, but Joe has a vivid memory of the ride there.

"I remember all four of us getting into a car. Our mother was there, and I know she was crying, and then we went from Truro to Halifax...and when we got to the orphanage, that's when we met [Mrs.] Patriquin."

After they entered the building, someone took them directly to the isolation room, where they stayed for several weeks.

Unlike other residents, who called it "the horror room," Joe was content to be there.

"When we were in Truro we were always hungry," he says. "And when we went to the orphanage we got fed. We had to eat everything that was put in front of us, but that was the great part: you weren't hungry anymore. So I thought that was great. Even though it might be horror for some people, to us, having nothing at all, it was really good."

But what happened the day they left the room made him wonder if that good feeling would last.

"I'll never forget this," he says, even though he lives many miles away, and it's been many decades since those moments when he first met the matron whose name he thinks he remembers, but isn't sure.

Other matrons took his sisters, Florence and Lillian, to a different part of the orphanage.

She took Joe and his brother, Ray, downstairs.

"There's a room, a locker room, where you can hang up your coats and put your shoes under," says Joe. "My number downstairs in the locker was number forty-eight; my brother was forty-seven...."

"She said, 'I want you to take off your jackets and hang them up.' I hung it up on forty-seven and I got a sting across my back; I looked around and she's there with a strap, and she whacked me right across the neck and back."

"That's not number forty-eight," the matron told Joe. "You hung your coat on forty-seven; now get it over there."

"And this was right at the beginning, and I thought, 'Oh my God.'"

That matron was the worst, he says, as were his first two years in the orphanage. Later, other events, like his summers at camp, Saturday trips to Roy Rogers movies, and other outings, started to eclipse the bad things that had happened there.

Bad things like the time matrons washed his mouth out with soap, and the time he was punished for trying to stop a matron from strapping a younger boy.

In the first case, Joe had stolen a jackknife from a Halifax store. The cashiers knew he was from the orphanage and reported him to staff. The matrons asked him if he'd stolen anything.

"I said I didn't, and they found it in my pocket," he recalls.

They took him to an upstairs bathroom and forced soap into his mouth for lying.

"They put it there and they take their hands and twist it around and it's got to be the worst tasting stuff in the world," he says. "You couldn't do anything. It just tasted terrible."

He takes part of the blame, though, acknowledging he had stolen and lied about it.

But he's less forgiving for what happened to other kids—routinely strapped at bedtime if their hands or their underwear were dirty. He could hear them crying.

Like others, he remembers then–head matron Sara Patriquin fondly. She was "the nicest lady," he says at one point. "When you walked by her, she was always smiling at you and stuff like that. The other ones would never look at you."

But, he says, Patriquin often oversaw the bedtime inspections and strapped the children, too.

"Before you went upstairs, you had to wash before you went to bed," he recalls. "Then when you were at the end of the bed, you had to show your hands, and then she would go through your underwear. If you had any [dirty] marks in there, you would get a whack with the strap. Yeah, you would get a hit. The belt too; she had a belt.

"That's every night; every night you had to do that. You had to wash up, stand at the end of the bed with your pajamas on."

Patriquin never hit Joe–"I was eight years old; I was pretty good," he says of keeping himself clean.

"And my brother was, too; he was in a bed next to me."

But another matron–he doesn't know who–once punished him in the middle of the night.

"I was hit once when a little boy came on board," he recalls.

"I think he was five years old, and he was crying. He came in; I guess he had no parents, or something happened to his parents. I don't know what it was; I never really got into it, but anyways, he was crying. My brother and I, we were about three beds away from this boy that was crying, and this matron come in and she said, 'Who's crying?'

"She put her flashlight in everybody's eyes, and she found the little boy that was crying, and she told him to stop crying. He started crying again, so she gave him a whack–she gave him two or three whacks—and I said to her, 'Isn't that enough, already?'

"You know, I'm only eight years old—and she whacked me.

"He was only five."

But, like Leonard Chater, Joe often recounts many of his own punishments with an air of inevitability and acceptance.

What was he thinking at the time? How did he cope with all these things as a boy?

"I don't know," he says. "I think that's the way life was for me. I never had anything better, you know. You get used to that kind of stuff."

He had to get used to the racial slurs, too—kids calling out "chinky, chinky Chinaman!" as he walked by. One day, one of them threw a rock-filled snowball that injured Joe's left eye. He wasn't blinded, but it affected his vision, so authorities sent him to the Halifax School for the Blind, where he stayed during the week. He lived in the orphanage on weekends.

Orphanage documents, which describe him as "a real nice boy, obedient and truthful," show he was transferred to the School for the Blind in the spring of 1953, and Joe wonders if his sparse memory of the orphanage rituals others describe might be because he spent so little time there from 1953 to 1955.

While his eye healed, Joe was expected to learn Braille in addition to his other studies. He struggled with both, as he would with academics in his later years, when he lived with foster parents and worked on their farm, leaving him no time to study. He was always behind, always feeling "stupid" compared to the other kids.

While at the School for the Blind, he continued to be, as the orphanage records call him, "a nice boy."

The school housed many Halifax Explosion survivors who had been blinded in the blast that also destroyed the first orphanage building on Veith Street.

"Because I could see, I used to take them to their appointments," Joe remembers. "Some of them,...[I'd] take them to get a glass eye fitted."

He walked to the school every Sunday night and returned to the orphanage each Friday afternoon, sometimes stopping at the corner store nearby. He and others pressed foil from candy bar wrappers into fake nickels and dimes, passing them off as real money to buy more treats.

"Until we got caught," Joe says. "Boy, we got the strap [then].

"But I deserved that," he says. "I deserved stuff like that, because you should never do it."

⋘ ◉ ⋙

JOE'S MOTHER

BY THIS TIME, Joe's biological mother had moved to Halifax too.

Sometimes, he and his brother walked downtown to visit her at her apartment on Grafton Street, where she lived with another man.

"My brother and I would be walking up to see her, and she'd be hanging out the window with the bottle, and just call us names—'What the F– are you doing up here?' But you know, days that she was good, she was good."

She was good if they could catch her before she started drinking, before they'd find her passed out on the floor, and they'd search for her cheap wine and pour it down the sink.

And she was good—sober—when she visited them in the orphanage.

"She was there three or four times, her and another Chinese guy. He was a nice man. They used to bring us bananas...and oranges and chocolate bars.

"When she came into the orphanage, it was the best thing that could ever happen to you. You'd feel it," he says. "You've got your mom there."

But that didn't last. His mother was an alcoholic "until the day she died," he says. He says he still feels sorry for her.

"Her whole family went against her."

Joe and his siblings rarely saw their mother after they left the orphanage and essentially became, as many children had through the years, child labour for their foster parents.

"You had to work twelve to sixteen hours every day when you're small like that," Joe says of his foster home in Stewiacke.

"Milking cows and cleaning and going to the woods on weekends and cutting down trees and stuff like that. We had to clean the barn...and put the manure on wheelbarrows and take it outside. It was continuous, for all day long. And we had to go to school, and then the minute you get out of school, you could never have time to study," says Joe. "You had to go and work and then the teacher wondered why you didn't know anything."

Joe had to take grade seven three times. He didn't graduate from high school. He stayed on the farm—"the worst place"—until he was eighteen, always missing those later years at the orphanage, when he'd had friends, and when the cook, Mrs. Fraser, gave him hugs and chocolate bars whenever she'd see him. And when they'd go to Roy Rogers and Gene Autry movies, and spend summers at the YMCA Big Cove Camp in Pictou County, where he learned to swim and row and make shelters in the woods.

Old newspaper clippings show Joe and other boys standing with fishing poles on the dock, learning about rose galls (round growths with spikes that form on rose stems) and about tying rope.

"It was great. You'd hate to come back," he says.

But later, he hated to leave.

"Yellow bastards," his foster mother and father called him and his siblings, Raymond, Lillian, and Florence. They were among the sixteen foster children the couple took in, who slept "two or three in a bed."

There would be little time then for games like the ones they used to play at the orphanage. No "red rover, red rover" or baseball or swimming in the wading pool—only brief, cherished moments playing with the farm dog, Tuggy. Old pictures show Joe smiling as he holds Tuggy's paws and hugs the black-and-white border collie.

"That's the dog that I loved," he says.

Most of the time, he and his siblings were working—in the woods, in the barn, in the house.

Their foster father often threatened them with sticks. Once, he slammed a broom against Joe's back when Joe teased their

Joe Gooey loved his foster parents' farm dog, Tuggy. *(Joe Gooey)*

adopted son—a favourite child who was treated differently than the others.

Joe, almost eighteen, was strong by then. He was used to loading sixty-pound milk cans on trucks, twenty-five at a time. He knew he'd be leaving soon, since the couple would no longer get paid to keep him when he became an adult.

So Joe grabbed the broom and tried to hit his foster father back, but his brother stopped him. Joe didn't get supper that night. Eventually, he left the foster parents who had been "terrible right to the end," as he put it.

"All they wanted [was] just us to work and work and work. Nothing else."

~°~

ON THE ROAD

AFTER JOE LEFT, he worked at other farms, but they neglected to pay him as promised.

Desperate, he decided to hitchhike to Ontario for work. It would be a harrowing two-week journey with little food or shelter.

He got a ride the day he left, but things took a turn for the worse after the truck driver dropped him off in New Brunswick. It was pitch dark and Joe was "in the middle of nowhere." All he had was a pillowcase stuffed with a few pieces of clothing, a carrot, and a potato he had taken from the back of the truck.

It was April 1962, and there was still snow on the ground. He slept outdoors, on the side of the highway, in the wet and the cold.

He looked dirty, he says, and no one would pick him up.

He walked for days until he saw the lights from a farmhouse on a hill two or three miles away. He climbed the hill and knocked on the door.

"I was starving; I had nothing....I was weak, I was tired, I was wet,...and I asked her for something to eat. She didn't understand me at all—apparently she was French—so she just pointed to me and she told me 'just wait,'" he recalls. "She had a daughter that could speak a little bit of English and I told her that I was hungry, and was there anything I could do [to] work for a meal? And she said, 'No, Mom will feed you.'"

They took him in and fed him sandwiches and gave him a lunch to take away. Not long afterward, a truck driver bound for Quebec gave him a ride.

But Joe didn't stay in Quebec long. He worked for a few days at a factory and slept on the ground in a park at night. But he couldn't understand the language or get permanent work, so he returned to Nova Scotia and worked more odd jobs before eventually leaving again for Ontario, where he stayed for good. He married the woman who would become his wife of almost fifty years, and became the father of two children. He worked his way up to inspector in the boiler company where he stayed for forty years.

Today, Joe says his life is good. He's retired now. He says his grown children and his grandchildren have never wanted for anything—a source of pride for a man who "started from scratch"—a man who "had nothing."

And he no longer longs for the things others have—as he had when the children down the road from the farm enjoyed houses full of Christmas presents every year. Now, he can get himself whatever he wants.

"I don't know why; I bought a lot of train sets," he says. "I bought a 1950 jukebox. I got gumball machines. I got everything that everybody would want. [I have] thousands of dollars' [worth] right here, right now.

"I don't know; it's something that I couldn't get when I was small.

"Now I've got it all."

Chapter Four: The Fortunate One
Sandy Murray

T HE TRAINS USED TO RUN beside the water. They
still do, down past the Halifax Shipyards.

And in Sandy Murray's mind.

They slow down, speed up, wind around–go all the way
back to the beginning.

Like his thoughts of Satan.

And his thoughts of his mother in her coffin.

And his thoughts of his brother, Laurie–"the Godfather of
the Orphanage"–long gone.

Laurie taught Sandy how to climb over the orphanage
fence; how to hide in the bushes by the tracks; how to wait for
the trains to slow down; how to jump up, hang on.

"Jump off, jump off!" Laurie yelled the first time, after
Sandy hung on too long, his leg too close to the wheel, the

train speeding up—barrelling away from a place that felt like "a jail."

Sandy jumped off, rolled onto the gravel, tore his shirt, skinned his knees. But he did it again.

For the fun. And the freedom.

And the chance to be away from a place of fear and order and control.

Sometimes the brothers ran away for a day. Sometimes they'd hide, with their orphanage buddies, in little wooden huts they made out of empty orange crates in the backyard.

"These were our security blankets," Sandy says. "Security blankets...from the matrons, the rules, the regulations. Our own space. We could do or say whatever we wanted.

"Of course they made us tear them down."

The boys longed for security during much of their childhood. Sandy, who spent months in the orphanage, sometimes found it. Laurie, who spent ten years in the orphanage, never could.

Most of Laurie's life there remains a mystery.

Sandy knows only fragments of that life—a life with "no love." Sandy's started that way, too, at least as far back as he can remember.

He was four, living with an elderly woman, her daughter, and her son on Quarry Road in Halifax—the first of two foster homes he lived in before he entered the orphanage in 1953.

Sandy thinks they were "holy rollers"—religious fanatics. "There was something not right with them," he says.

A few scattered images have stayed with him for seventy years: he walks into their home. He plays on the floor with a little boy, whose mother gives him cereal. He's stung by bees; they put mud on his swollen skin. They're renovating their house, but tell him, "You're not going to be here" when it's finished.

They lock him in a bathroom, go outside, and scrape rakes against the walls.

He's scared all the time.

"I was scared of Satan," Sandy says. "That's what they put into my head—that Satan was everywhere."

It stayed in his head even after a black car showed up—"like you see in the movies"—and a Children's Aid worker took him away. He was upset. He may have cried.

"I remember looking out the back window seeing this lady and her son...and basically I was going. I didn't know where I was going, but I was going."

❧ ⊙ ❧

MRS. MORRIS

SANDY WAS GOING to what would be a better place, to live with a woman he calls "Mrs. Morris" now, but called "Nanny" then. For most of his life, he didn't even know her first name, learning only recently that it was Catherine.

She would play a pivotal "loving" role in Sandy's life—then and later.

But at first, he was frightened. "Petrified," he says.

"I go into the house....I hide under the kitchen table. Mrs. Morris is trying to get me to come out; I won't come out. Her daughter worked at the Dominion store on Quinpool Road, [and she] came home with some of the girls from work to see this new foster child. Basically, they talked me out from under the table maybe with a few pennies or something."

But that night he was still terrified. "Mrs. Morris, even then–she tried to comfort me," he says. She brought him upstairs to "a very small room," maybe meant for a baby, with a dresser and a bed, so tight she could barely open the door.

She turned off the light.

"God, no! Don't turn off the light! No, no, I'm scared!" he remembers crying.

"Okay," she said. "I'll leave the light on."

"She went downstairs and then she came back up again and she turned the light out. Well, in the middle of the night I got up and went into her room, and she allowed me to...sleep beside her.

"That was good, except what happened was, she decided she was going to break me of that habit because I was doing it every night, and she says, 'No, you have to stay in your room.'"

But Sandy snuck out anyway, went into her room, lay on the cedar chest by her bed, and pulled the rug off the floor for a blanket.

His fear came out in other ways, like when Mrs. Morris wanted to take him to the movies.

"Satan's in the movies," he told her.

"So Satan, from my perspective–Satan was in the movies, Satan was–if you turned the lights off, Satan was everywhere.

"But years later I loved going to the movies. Satan disappeared. I got rid of Satan."

Sandy—whose given name is Allison Murray—didn't have any awareness of his birth parents during his early days with Mrs. Morris on Oak Street, in a house that still stands today.

He first saw his mother many years later, in her coffin.

He first saw his father, when he was five, on his way home from grade one at Sir Charles Tupper Elementary School. A taxi pulled up beside him and the driver rolled down his window. He asked if he was Allison Murray.

"I said yes, and he says, 'Well, I'm your father.'"

Mrs. Morris had warned Sandy not to talk to strangers, so he ran home—but his father followed. His father had seen his picture in a local newspaper, which used to run class photographs of children who were starting school.

He asked Mrs. Morris if he could sometimes visit his son. She agreed.

Sandy Murray's foster mother—a woman he knew only as "Mrs. Morris" or "Nanny"—played a pivotal and loving role in Sandy's life. She's shown here with her husband, who died before Sandy came to live with her. *(Sandy Murray)*

His father told him he had brothers and sisters. He took him out for haircuts. He bought him new shoes—Sandy's were so worn he had to put pieces of cardboard in the soles.

"At that stage he was a very gentle, caring, loving father," he says.

Sandy would often smell alcohol on his father's breath, but he didn't know what that meant. He learned later that his father—a veteran of two world wars, husband to a woman in a psychiatric hospital, father of fourteen children—was an alcoholic. Sandy imagined what "tough choices" he must have had to make.

"But that's a different story," he says.

Sandy stayed on Oak Street until he was ten. These were the days of comic book heroes like Superman and Plastic Man and movie ingenue Doris Day and radio-show detective Boston Blackie—"an enemy to those who make him an enemy; a friend to those who have no friend."

Sandy was wild back then, a "bad, bad kid," despite the influence of "a fantastic woman" whose kindness still makes him tear up when he thinks of how he stole from her and lied to her—and how she took care of him anyway.

He and his best friend roamed the streets, lighting fires, stealing comics, stealing Pez candy and jackknives, and training younger children to steal for them. Sometimes he stole Mrs. Morris's milk money for movies and snacks.

"Give him a crack or something," her youngest adult daughter—one of five, but the only one who still lived at home—used to say.

"He's going to have enough cracks in his life," Mrs. Morris would reply.

"So, she only hit me once," Sandy says. "The reason she hit me is because I stole some money from her....

"That's a very important one....I was still at that stage she'd every once in a while let me sleep in her bed. Or on a Sunday night, we'd be listening to Boston Blackie on the radio and I'd fall asleep. Anyway she'd gone downstairs and she had left this money on her dresser. I don't know if it was for laundry or whatever," he says.

"I got out of bed, saw it, and I stole it."

He met up with his best friend and they went to the drugstore, where he used the money to buy them both jackknives. Then they went to a restaurant and had breakfast. Then they went to the movie theatre.

"I'm standing in line at the Oxford Theatre...and Mrs. Morris comes walking down and she calls me out; she says, 'Did you steal any money?' and of course I said no, and she said, 'What's that lovely knife hanging off of you?'

"She marched me back to every place...trying to get her money back, because money was tight."

Mrs. Morris took Sandy home and sent him upstairs for her hairbrush. She gave him "a couple of cracks" on his rear end. And then she went to the telephone and threatened to call Children's Aid and send him to the orphanage.

"I just broke down crying. I swore I'd never do anything again," he says. "So that's, like, a big event, because I felt, in my case, a guilt thing about her being so good and me being so bad."

❦

"MEET YOUR BROTHER"

MRS. MORRIS DIDN'T send Sandy to the orphanage then, but that was about to come. Not because he was bad, but because she was sick. Sandy didn't know it then, but she had been diagnosed with cancer. He thinks Mrs. Morris, her daughters, and the Children's Aid workers developed a plan to gradually introduce him to the orphanage.

"How would you like to meet your brother?" one of the social workers asked one day after taking him to a routine medical appointment.

"I said, 'Oh yeah, I'd love to meet my brother.'"

He didn't know anything about his brother Laurie or where he lived.

When the social worker took him to the orphanage, Laurie was down the street playing basketball in a church gym. They went to the gym and the game stopped. Laurie came over and introduced himself. Then they went to the orphanage, where Sandy saw a big yard and swings and a wading pool.

An interesting kind of place, he thought.

It was just a visit, but that soon changed.

"So here's the strategy," he says. "So then she says to me, 'How would you like to spend a weekend?'—the lady from the Children's Aid—and you've got to remember this is all being orchestrated....They're trying to make this transition.

"So what happened was, I was spending the weekend with my brother in the orphanage and I was coming home, and finally it happened that I was spending the week in the orphanage and coming home on the weekend. So at some point there, I'm not coming home at all."

A 1953 Ladies' Committee report verifies the plan: "Sandy Murray who has been spending week-ends at the Home with his brother Laurie, will be admitted as soon as school closes to the Home and will also go to camp with Laurie."

At some point–like other new residents through the years–Sandy spent time in "the horror room," although he doesn't call it that.

The quarantine room was meant to prevent lice or rashes or other conditions from spreading, but as others have recalled, it was also a scary, isolating introduction to a scary, isolating place.

Sandy remembers being in the room by himself.

"It was lonely....There was no bathroom in there. I couldn't even tell you how I went to the bathroom," he says. "I think they locked the door."

It left a mark.

"Think about somebody that's been living with somebody, and suddenly being locked in a room by themselves at ten years old," Sandy says. "It's trauma. It has an impact on you. It leaves an emotional scar."

When Sandy got out of the isolation room, his brother Laurie tried to protect him.

"He comes to me one day and he says, 'Look, if this matron'–whose name I don't know–'comes after you, she's going to have a yardstick. I want you to run down the hall here, and then I want you to turn around fast, grab that yardstick out of her hand, and snap it over your knee....'

"So I don't know what I was doing; anyway, one of the matrons comes down with her yardstick. She's chasing me; I'm running; suddenly I get the flashback of what Laurie told me. I turn around, I grab this damn yardstick—which was a thicker one—snapped it. It made a hell of a racket. This matron took off, going the other way. Oh, yeah—scared the living hell out of her.

"See, my brother knew—because he had done it, probably—he knew how the system worked."

Sandy started calling Laurie "The Godfather of the Orphanage" because he'd been there so long—since he was seven. Laurie stayed until he was sixteen or seventeen. He was never adopted or taken in by foster parents.

He knew how the system worked and found ways around it, but he was still a child—just a few years older than Sandy. He regularly wet the bed. Sandy is convinced—although he never witnessed it—that Laurie was abused.

But he helped to make sure Sandy wasn't—even found ways to make Sandy's life in the orphanage fun.

"My brother was very creative," Sandy says. "He caught a grass snake; he used to sleep with a grass snake and I slept [in a bed] beside him....

"He got a *Popular Mechanics* and he found a crystal radio, and when they would let us out to go to a movie, we would go in and steal various parts for that crystal radio, because we knew the inventory of what we needed.

"So we built the crystal radio—or he did. [We had] Air Force headsets and we had an antenna we'd throw that out the window, and then everybody would take a little turn listening to the radio. So that was pretty good."

So were the summer evenings when, for reasons Sandy still doesn't understand, he was allowed to stay up late with his brother and the other older boys, instead of going to bed at six o'clock with his peers.

So were the nights in the dorm when one of the boys stole a key to the pantry, took everyone's orders, snuck down, and brought up snacks.

So were the train rides, even that first time.

The brothers and other orphanage boys waited in the bushes for the train to slow down. His brother showed him what to do and jumped aboard. Sandy followed.

"My leg's swinging right under by the wheel. I could have lost my leg," he says.

"I'm hanging on the side of the car and the train is starting to pick up speed. My brother has jumped off, and I go by him and he's yelling to me: 'Jump off, jump off!' So the train is going like a bat out of hell; I jump off and I roll, and I've got just a white T-shirt on, and I think I had short pants on....My shirt is torn; I've got blood all over my knees."

But it was exhilarating, and he did it again, sometimes on his own—running away for a day, just like he and Laurie had done when a prospective adoptive mother took them to her home.

"On Sundays...people could come to visit you, or if they were thinking of trying to have you become a foster child or adopted, they would have somebody come and pick you up and take [you] to [their] home. So...they said they'd like to keep the two brothers together, and this woman was prepared to do that.

"She took us to her house in Spryfield; we sit down at the table, she gives us something to eat—Laurie's at one end of the table; I'm at the other. He looks at me. He says, 'Do you like this woman?'

"I said no. She comes back into the room. He says, 'Can we go outside and play?' She says, 'Yes, but just stay close to the house.'

"Well, you've got to remember, we've been under lock and key—you let us out, we're gone. We were gone—we took off. We went to the store; we stole some gum and candy, you know—we just had a field day, and we knew she had to have us back by, say, five o'clock. We didn't come back 'til, like, four-thirty. This woman was having a nervous breakdown. She was so glad to get rid of us and take us back to the orphanage."

⌇⌇⌇

DESPERATION

BUT SANDY WASN'T happy to be back in the orphanage. He missed Mrs. Morris, and he missed his freedom.

The matrons ruled with "authority," he says.

And "there was definitely fear," he remembers. "When you're a child, you have no power."

He thinks of a boy he once saw in a cage. And another, on the roof.

The cage, he thinks, was a punishment room—with chicken wire, "like a jail"—inside the orphanage. "It definitely was some kind of lock-up." But it's just a flash of a memory, with no context before or after, like the rakes scraping the walls, and the bee sting, and the black car taking him away when he was four.

The child on the roof is clearer.

"He was saying to us all week that his brother was in the navy and his brother was going to come, and he was going to get him out of the orphanage, and everybody was really pleased for him, and he was happy that week. I can't tell you how happy he was," Sandy says.

"I was down the bottom bringing in the milk or something, and I looked up and this kid is sitting on one of the windows getting ready to jump out. So I go up the stairs and...I remember talking to him, and he looked out the harbour and he saw his brother's ship going, and he knew that his brother wasn't going to come and get him.

"I talked this kid down out of the window. This kid turned into stone, like, they couldn't handle him," Sandy says. "If they couldn't control you, couldn't deal with you, you went to reform school—and he went to reform school."

Sandy's desperation was less stark, but he was determined to escape the place he calls "destructive" to a child's psyche and a child's soul.

"I hated it," he says. "It's like prison because, you've got to remember, the place is totally fenced, and it's a routine, you know? You get up, you clean up the bed, you get yourself dressed, you go down to the dining room,...you have your breakfast,...you feed the other kids,...you serve the stuff to the younger ones—so it's a whole routine....

"Here's a boy ten years old...that has total freedom, and [he feels like] the man of the house, running wild—doing whatever the hell he wants, really taking advantage of a situation: an elderly lady that...basically couldn't control me," he says.

"You take that person and you suddenly put him under lock and key—you're going to build up some resentment."

Sandy's resentment grew as the days passed; he longed for home.

He would stand behind the orphanage fence, and sometimes Mrs. Morris's daughter, who worked at the shipyards, stopped by.

"She would save me some of her lunch and I'd put my hand through the fence and she'd give it to me. And then the people in my neighbourhood, they would save some of their lunch for me. The thing about it was that I'm looking at this, thinking, 'Wait; they're going home.'

One night, he ran away. He'd been up late, out in the yard with his brother, when one of the matrons yelled at him to come inside.

"I always stay out with my brother," he told her.

"You get in here right away," she ordered.

Sandy turned to his brother. "I'm running away. Don't you squeal on me," he said.

"So off I go. I run all the way over to the lady's house that worked at the shipyards, one of the Morris daughters....I ran all the way up those hills,...and I ran all the way over to Willow Street....I'm running from the orphanage almost to Quinpool Road and never stopped. So I get there; I collapse in...the kitchen."

Mrs. Morris's daughter called the orphanage and the orphanage called the police, and they took him back to the building, where his brother waited.

"I get to the front door....The stairway has got all the kids on it. My brother's at the bottom of the stairway, and I walked

up to him and I said, 'You squealed on me, didn't you?' and...
he said, 'Yes, I did, but I love you.' And off we went upstairs to
the dormitory."

But Sandy didn't stay.

"You'll never keep me in here," he kept telling Children's
Aid workers and the matrons, whose names he doesn't
remember, because, he says, "We were just kids...you get
mental blocks; your system just doesn't want to remember."

"I want to go home," he kept telling them.

And eventually, he did.

Mrs. Morris, still ill, took him back, provided he would be
able to go to Big Cove—a children's wilderness and leadership
camp in Pictou County, Nova Scotia—during the summer
months.

"So I went back home," he says, and he stayed home for
almost four years.

He was still a "bad bugger" he says. And "mean." He stole.
He got into fights with other kids who made fun of him for
being "adopted." He pulled pranks at school, littering the
grounds and trees with toilet paper, filling a water gun with ink
and etching "Zorro" on the bathroom wall.

"I used to get the strap all the time [at school]," Sandy says.
And despite the love he received at home, he still felt like an
outsider.

"You're totally different; you're outside the universe of the
normal family."

⚜

"FAMILY"

SANDY'S KNOWLEDGE OF his biological family unfolded gradually. A turning point came when he was twelve, skating on a rink in the backyard on Oak Street.

Mrs. Morris came out and brought him into the house.

"Your mother died," she told him.

"Oh, okay," he said. And went back to skating.

But it hit him later. "My mother died," he blurted when he went to his friend's house. And he started crying.

"I have no idea why," he says. "I'd never met my mother."

When he got to school, he cried again and the teacher sent him home.

His family told Mrs. Morris that Sandy's brothers and sisters would be at the funeral home. So Sandy went, too–his first time meeting some of them, and his first memory of his mother.

"I go up and look at my mother in the coffin, and that's the first time I ever saw her," he says.

"So these are emotional turmoils in the soul."

The image has stayed with him, even though he didn't feel an emotional attachment to her then, and doesn't feel one now.

But he thinks of her, and his father. His brothers. His days in the orphanage. His days on Oak Street. And beyond.

Sandy became a ward of Children's Aid in 1947 after his mother had a breakdown and entered a psychiatric hospital. She spent eight years there–first at the Nova Scotia Hospital,

Sandy Murray's mother, Deleta Murray. *(Sandy Murray)*

Sandy Murray's father, Thomas Murray. *(Sandy Murray)*

then at the Halifax County Home and Mental Hospital. She died in 1955.

He's created short videos on Facebook with pictures and stories about the people he knew, and the people he didn't. In colour. And in black and white.

In one photo, his mother is wearing a dark, high-collared coat and a fascinator-style hat—reminiscent of royalty. She has dark hair and dark eyes. She looks to the side, half-smiling as though she has a secret.

His father is standing in his First World War uniform, holding a bugle. He joined at seventeen. He served again in the Second World War. And somewhere in between, he met Deleta and they eventually had fourteen children; two died in infancy.

Then his wife got sick and he sent his children to orphanages and to foster homes—in Sandy's case, first for a few years with his mother's relatives in Dover, when Sandy was too little to have any memories.

Sandy Murray, age twelve, with his cat, Sailor.
(Sandy Murray)

Sandy has pictures of trains too, and of the house on Oak Street. And a picture of himself in grade one outside his school, and one of himself at age twelve in his backyard, wearing a bow tie and a hat and holding his cat, Sailor, who greeted him at the end of the street every day after school.

And a picture of Mrs. Morris, with her curly hair and a slight smile, standing with her husband, who died before she took Sandy in.

Sandy laughs often when retelling stories of his youth. The pranks. The scrapes with authority. The trips to Big Cove Camp, where he briefly saw Laurie again after he left the orphanage, and they peeled potatoes together by the campfire.

And the thrilling, sometimes dangerous, adventures with his best friend and his brother so many years ago.

He's jovial about the good and he's fatalistic about the bad. "I'm just one of the clowns," he says. "The world is kind of like a big circus."

But sometimes he stops and catches his breath.

Through hours of reminiscing Sandy starts to cry just twice: when he talks about stealing from Mrs. Morris and when he talks about her final gift to him, before she died.

"I'm in her bedroom where I used to sleep against the wall, because the bed was right against the wall. I was in there; I was crying. She's at home; she's...about to die. One of the daughters came in and said to me, 'Why are you crying?' And I said, 'She's going to die, and I'm going to have to go back to the orphanage.'

"She goes in; talks to her mother. Her mother calls me in—this is sad—she has all her daughters, five daughters, she makes them all promise that [they] will never send me back to the orphanage."

His voice cracks. And he pauses for a moment.

"That's a tough one."

That was 1957, when he was fourteen.

꒦ꙥꙥ

BREAKDOWNS

SOON SANDY STARTED "road trip living, with all the different mothers or daughters."

He lived in Cole Harbour, and in Shad Bay. In Liverpool and in Bridgewater. And eventually, back on Oak Street after Mrs. Morris's youngest daughter got married and had children and moved into her mother's home.

They all kept "the promise," and Sandy is grateful.

But, it was "a pretty complicated thing to be happening to you," he says.

"They have their own kids; they love their kids more than they love you, and you're a bit of a pain in the ass, so anyway it's like a second fiddle," he says. "None of them mistreated me; they all took very good care of me, but the reality was—it was a tough road to haul."

It had been a tough road for a long time. And eventually, because of a strange convergence of events, it caught up with him.

Sickness and his upbringing—maybe even his family's history of mental illness—merged into a harrowing and life-changing event Sandy suffered through then, but is grateful for now.

As their mother had been, Sandy's brothers Gus, Warren, and Earl, were all eventually hospitalized for what he calls "breakdowns."

And then Sandy was hospitalized, too.

He'd already moved with a different Morris daughter to Ottawa and had finished school there. Thanks to a good teacher in high school, he straightened up his attitude and his marks. But he got sick—physically and emotionally—at age twenty-one when he came back to his Halifax home to visit, and to bring Christmas presents to the children in the orphanage.

Sandy's appendix ruptured and they rushed him to hospital. Doctors operated, and when he woke up he started to hallucinate. He saw a white light; he saw nuns standing over him, even though it wasn't a Catholic hospital. He was having "an out-of-body experience."

"I go back to stay with the [Morris family] while I was waiting to get a plane to go back to Ottawa, and I start having problems with my mind," he says. "I just lose control of it. I basically get on a plane, and I get back to Ottawa, get in bed, and I'm going insane....I've got these thoughts of godliness. I'm picking up children. I'm holding them. I'm saying all kinds of religious stuff—just mindboggling."

He ended up in the Ottawa Sanitarium, a psychiatric hospital, where he stayed for about eight months.

For the first three days, Sandy lay on the floor, crying. He lost his ability to count and to communicate.

"You're like a child," he says, but "you're twenty-one years old."

Sandy gradually worked his way back to health. He'd forgotten many things, but not how to paint—a lifelong love that remains. "I painted my way back to sanity," he says.

And eventually, he was "reborn"—not in a religious sense, but because he got to begin again.

"I was lucky to have a nervous breakdown," he says. "That was the best thing that ever happened to me because it saved my soul. I mean, I had the guilt....The way I treated Mrs. Morris....My system was weakened, and, you know, my ability to fight the battles that I had fought, and the things I had done and seen....

"You know nothing; you have to come back from square one."

❧⊙❧

"A HEALTHIER ME"

SANDY WENT ON to a long and successful career in computer technology, working for some top companies, and later teaching at various schools, sometimes serving as principal. He got married and he had children and he came back—all the way.

"Back," he says, "as a healthier me."

"If I had continued on the road that I was on, I might have had a nervous breakdown like my brothers did when they were married. They waited longer. They battled the battle in their lives for a lot longer.

"I was fortunate; I got the healing and the health at twenty-one."

Fortunate. He repeats the word.

Fortunate he found Mrs. Morris.

Fortunate he wasn't beaten much in the orphanage.

Fortunate his life wasn't as bad as it was for some of the other boys—like the boy in the cage and the boy on the roof.

And fortunate that he had Laurie—the brother he was "close to, in a very strange way, for a very short time"—whose name appears in several old orphanage records, offering a brief glimpse into a boyhood that is mostly unknown.

In one old document, the Ladies' Committee praises Laurie's actions and altruism on a cold January day in the 1950s when the orphanage sprinklers leaked and the firefighters came, "and the children lined up quietly at the entrance to the fire escape door and waited to be told what to do.

"It was very realistic with our own bell ringing wildly etc.," the Ladies' Committee writes. "Laurie Murray who was in his bath at the time put on his trousers and rushed to the hospital room where he was met by Florence Gooey [Joe Gooey's sister], they both [started] to carry the sick children to the fire escape. This action was entirely unsolicited."

And another glimpse, in an old photo on Sandy's Facebook page. Laurie is a young man now, wearing a suit and tie and a white boutonniere. Confetti sprinkles his dark, slicked-back hair and his shoulders. He looks away from the camera. This may have been Laurie's wedding day, but Sandy isn't sure.

Laurie had joined the Air Force when he got out of the orphanage, but he punched an officer and received a dishonourable discharge.

Sandy Murray called his brother Laurie (shown here) "The Godfather of the Orphanage" because he'd been there so long. *(Sandy Murray)*

"He was a risk-taker," Sandy says. "He lived on the razor's edge. He raced cars. He did everything that was dangerous."

He became "a stranger" to Sandy, who named one of his daughters Laurie, after the boy who was "never hugged" and "never loved."

"His life was awful. I mean—I was fortunate. At least I was a foster child. He was an orphan," Sandy says. "Never adopted, never a foster child. Nobody showed him any love."

Sandy spoke to Laurie one last time, on the phone, before he died. Laurie was thirty-eight, in the hospital after a heart attack.

"He said to me, 'I always wanted to go to Dalhousie University,' so he donated his body to Dalhousie University Medical [School]."

Laurie Murray was buried in Dover—in the same grave as the mother he had never known.

Chapter Five:
"One Boy"
Paul Sabarots

T HE HEART TATTOO ON HIS arm has faded. The words "Mom" and "Dad" have been erased by time.

Paul Sabarots got the tattoo when he was thirteen, after he left the orphanage and went to a foster home.

He stretches out his right forearm and points to where the letters used to be. And a family that never was.

"The worst thing I ever did in my life," he says.

"It used to say 'Mom' and 'Dad'—now isn't that ironic? I don't have a mother, I don't have a father, but that's the tattoo I picked...and it spoke to me."

His parents were alive at the time, but he didn't know his father.

"My mother," Paul says, "didn't want me, so she gave me up as a ward of the Children's Aid."

That was more than fifty years ago.

Paul is in his early sixties now, sitting in the cozy, happy Lower Sackville home he shares with his wife, Trudy. He's surrounded by pictures of his children and grandchildren and the half-sisters he discovered just a few years ago.

But the past isn't far behind.

It never is.

As a child, Paul lived in two orphanages, twenty-one foster homes, and a reform school for boys. Before that, he lived with his alcoholic grandmother and an aunt, whom he thinks of as his sister. After that, he lived in a haze of heroin and other addictions before he quit for good and rose above other people's low expectations.

Paul Sabarots, shown here on the day of his First Communion in May 1964, lived as a child in two orphanages, twenty-one foster homes, and a reform school for boys. *(Paul Sabarots)*

As he talks about it all, Paul's mind is a whirlwind of beatings and ridicule, rejection and struggle, even if he can't always remember the exact times or dates or names of the people who hurt him.

"My life is all broken up in pieces," he says, thinking of the scattered documents he's found that tell only part of his story, from people who never knew him but called him "delinquent" and "trouble"–but got at least one thing right: "Paul is... looking for acceptance...[and] a stable family unit," he once read.

"I never found that," he says today. At least, not as a child. Like others who lived in the orphanage, Paul's life before and after was a desperate search for love, and relentless struggle for survival. Pieces of his past emerge in brief, indelible pictures.

Taking his wagon to get bags of coal at the store.

Seeing his grandmother drunk in her bed when he returned.

Dodging the empty wine bottles she'd throw in a drunken rage.

Stealing food because he was hungry.

Enduring beatings by nuns in a Catholic orphanage.

Enduring beatings by matrons in the Protestant orphanage.

Enduring beatings by foster parents, in home after home after home.

✐ ◉ ✐

GRANDMOTHER

PAUL'S FIRST "PARENT"–long before he went into the Protestant orphanage in 1967–was his grandmother.

She didn't beat him. But she didn't take care of him either.

"I have absolutely no memory whatsoever of my grandmother ever cooking," he says. "Most of the time when she would [get] a cheque or whatever, it was off to the liquor store and we fended for ourselves....

"There was never food in the house. Like, I'd go over to the liquor store and wait for the fish truck to come by delivering mackerel or selling mackerel and that outside. [I'd] distract him and grab a couple of mackerel and I was gone."

Paul would cook them in their apartment when he was only seven or eight years old.

Or he'd go to the corner store and steal cakes and pop and chips—"Whatever you could when you were hungry."

He was hungry "a lot."

And they moved a lot—to the "poor" areas of Halifax, where his grandmother would get into fights with her neighbours—"down on the ground," he says. "I mean, clothes flying and everything."

She got kicked out for not paying the rent.

She came home with strange men.

"When you're addicted to any type of substance, it gets to a point where there's nothing you won't do to get it. I've been there myself—I know that. My grandmother was at the point many times where we'd come home and there would be a different man in the house drinking with her and whatever," Paul says.

"I don't remember any Christmases whatsoever, any occasions whatsoever."

His only comfort was the "terrific man" his grandmother lived with for a time, before he couldn't take it anymore. He had a dent along his skull from a wine bottle she once threw at him.

He was Paul's only father figure—a man he still refers to as his "father"—who stayed in his life. Later, he helped save Paul's life.

When he wasn't at home, Paul went to Saint Mary's Boys' School on Grafton Street, where he faced different humiliations; he started fighting with other kids when he was just five years old.

"I look back now and I think I'd definitely do things different[ly], but I mean, we can sit here tomorrow and say I would have [done] things different yesterday, too.

"This guy started making fun of me because I had clothes that his mother had donated to the church....My grandmother would take us up to the church...to pick out something to wear, because all the money that was given to her for clothes or whatever went to liquor, and that would be the first fight I could remember—fist fight.

"He started making fun of me because I was wearing second-hand clothes; just called me names like bum and...beggar," Paul says.

"Of course I get thrown out of school....A few months later, I had to get glasses, and of course welfare was paying for them. They gave me pink-rimmed round glasses. I'm going to school and other kids are starting to make fun of them. They used to have the trolleys going up and down Spring Garden Road with the two rails," he says. "I remember the bus coming by, and I thought, 'Okay, nobody's making fun of me anymore.' And I took the glasses off and I put them under the tire, then I went and had a fight with them."

⚜

THE CATHOLIC ORPHANAGE

PAUL LAUGHS SOMETIMES, talking about the schoolyard fights and some of his other experiences living with relatives— strange experiences that seemed normal at the time.

Like the time welfare couldn't find them yet another place to live, so they stayed with old people in a nursing home next door to Rockhead Prison, where Paul would shimmy up a tree and sit on the wall and talk to the prisoners in striped uniforms as they raked potatoes.

But things were about to get a lot worse, and soon he started feeling like a prisoner, too.

By 1965 or '66 his grandmother's boyfriend had moved out. He still visited Paul from time to time, but he couldn't stop her drinking or her wild behaviour, which had gotten progressively worse.

"We were living on Bloomfield Street in the north end of Halifax, and we had the upstairs flat. The house is still there," he says. "That's when Children's Aid got involved, because my grandmother had to go into the Nova Scotia Hospital for what they considered shock treatment back then. They would try to shock the devil out of you with electricity. I believe that was the first time I went to the orphanage."

First, he went to St. Joseph's Catholic Orphanage; he thinks he stayed for about two years, but isn't sure, since, "as a child, time is also distorted.

"Your timeline gets messed up," he says, and there are still "a lot of spaces in the past."

But he remembers his first day in the Catholic facility. His aunt and a social worker walked him there, stopping at a corner store to buy him a bag of Smarties.

"I knew something was up," he says with a laugh, "because we didn't have money to buy Smarties."

He says he has "very bad" memories of the Catholic orphanage. "There was a lot of abuse."

He can still see the nuns in their long, dark robes and their habits—"all proper"—welcoming him while his aunt (who he thought of as his sister) and the social worker were still there. "The minute my sister and the social worker walked out the door, it was like night and day."

One of those nights is seared into his memory.

"I got my ass beat," Paul says.

"They had two dorms; one for the boys, one for the girls, and they had nuns sleeping on either side....They had their little room down in the corner. She came out, went to the bathroom—one of the nuns. I could hear her walking, and when she came back, I sat up in bed to look—that was my big mistake. You were never allowed to see a nun without her habit. I got that leather strap so hard that my ass bled."

Many more beatings followed, multiple times a week, on his bare behind and on other parts of his body, he says.

"They'd strap you over the desk...usually down in the head nun's office," Paul recalls.

"It seemed like it was never done where you could see it. It was across the back or the rear end...where if someone were to come in and look at you, they'd think, 'Well, they're just a little kid.' They don't see the bruising underneath. So a lot of it was done so it was protecting the people who did it," he says.

"I got to the point where I was getting tired of being beat three or four times a week....They'd say 'Okay, everyone go down and get your boots and hat on,' or whatever. If you were too slow doing it, you got it then. If you were eating and you didn't like what you were eating, you got it. A very, very strict regimen. Very strict.

"I would complain to my father [his grandmother's ex-boyfriend] and my sister [his aunt] all the time.

"But...the times were different. Nowadays, if a child went to the police, [if] a patrol car drives by and a child goes up to the car and says, 'Oh my God, I was just beat by this guy,' you'd have fifteen cars there in less than five minutes. Back then, you could have [gone] to a judge and they'd look at you and say, 'That never happened.'

"It got to the point where I fought back—[I'd] curse and swear at them.

"The more you curse and the more you swear, the more they'd try to hit you. And you'd get tired of that. And one day I struck one of the nuns," Paul recalls. "I was told I had to go down and get my punishment. I said, 'No, you've punished me for the last time.'

"I believe they requested I leave, and I think within twenty-four hours they put me in...the Protestant orphanage."

CRೀ ◎ ⌒ೀ

THE PROTESTANT ORPHANAGE

A SOCIAL WORKER with Children's Aid took Paul to the
Protestant Orphanage in 1967.

And now matrons were the ones holding the straps and
making the rules.

"I had it done so many times, I can't remember which ones
it was," he says of the women who repeatedly strapped him on
his bare bum.

Or hit him with wooden paddles.

Or punished him in other ways.

"I used to have to scrub the stairs a lot–iron stairs on the
back of the building," he says. "Many a times I was there with
a toothbrush cleaning, because I cursed at a matron or I didn't
listen to what I was being told, or because they caught me
smoking or fooling around with one of the girls or whatever,
because there was a lot of that. You wouldn't think there would
be, but there was."

Matrons held him down on his bed when he wouldn't go
to sleep. "They would have two or three of them come in and
hold me down," Paul remembers.

And he recalls that "they would strap people to the bed," but
Paul can't describe the restraints other residents remember,
and he isn't sure if they used them on him, too.

"It's so hard to look back, you know," he says, sighing. "As
a child, you go through it, but then as you get older you block
it out. It's like the beatings. I can remember getting beat; I

couldn't tell you how long a period it was each time, or what person did it, but there was the memory....

"Names don't mean a lot," he adds, "because, basically... if one person is doing the punishment and three people are watching, all you see is four people doing the punishment....

"Watching is the same as doing, as far as I'm concerned."

And, he says, most, though not all of them, went along with these and other routines and punishments, including the mealtime rituals that have stayed with him—as they have stayed with other children of the 1950s and '60s like Linda Gray-LeBlanc and Joan Wilson. Wilson came to the orphanage a year after Paul, and she sat for hours at the dinner table as a reprimand for not eating all of her food.

Paul was punished for that too.

"They thought by sitting there for the next three hours that you were going to eat it—and, of course, me being from where I came from, my stubbornness was more than what they could handle—so I just sat there and said, 'Fine, we'll sit here for the next eight hours; it doesn't bother me,' and they'd get mad," he says. "And you weren't allowed to talk—like, anyone that walked through, the kids or whatever, weren't allowed to acknowledge you. You were like you weren't there physically, so no one was allowed to talk to you. And they'd keep you there for hours sometimes....

"I spent so many times doing that that it's all one."

The shaming—dinnertime humiliations, paddling, strapping—often took place in front of others. They also faced these kinds of public spectacles from neighbourhood children, who could see them playing in the fenced orphanage yard.

"They would walk by and they would say, 'Oh, you animals; you're stuck in the cage!'...They'd fire rocks at us; they'd fire anything they could fire at us and play dodgeball with us, more or less. You had to be ducking back and forth, because there was six or eight of them out there. They'd be calling, 'There's the orphan!' 'You're poor!' and this and that. 'You're in a cage where you belong!'" he remembers.

"I'm surprised to this day that I'm not dead, because there'd be six or eight of them out there and I'd be the only one jumping over the fence. I'd say, 'Come on, bring all six of you!' and I'd get in fights. Oh, my God—constantly."

At that time, between the ages of eleven and thirteen, Paul was one of the oldest in the orphanage. He was tough on the outside—armour earned from having to fight "to survive" for as long as he could remember.

But it wore him down.

"Without even realizing it—you only realize it years later—but you were losing your self-esteem minute by minute, because no matter where you went—if you went to school and you did something wrong in school, the teacher wouldn't come and say, 'Ok, Paul, you did that wrong.' It was like, 'You piece of junk; you piece of shit—you did this wrong.' Smack you, you know? Because I think, growing up back then as an orphan...I get the feeling that everybody was sort of obligated to treat you that you were no good; that you were garbage. Even the teachers.

"And you go into a store—we used to have a store on the corner of Young and Devonshire Avenue; it was a yellow building—and you'd go in and [the owner] would say, 'Get out of here, you orphan.'

"Of course, we were always stealing from him," Paul acknowledges with a laugh.

But he sees that, too, as behaviour born of his background, and of his life on the fringes of a society that saw children in his circumstances as "less than" others, and not deserving of the same compassion and care.

"If you were an orphan, you had to be treated a certain way" by police, by teachers, by matrons, by neighbours, by the churches—both Protestant and Catholic.

"It went like dominoes," he says.

"Back then...the Catholic Church ruled the world, and it's really baffling because the Catholic Church is supposed to be [about] look[ing] after your fellow man," Paul says. "They would all go to church, and you'd see them with their little bonnets on and their prayer books in their hands, but then the minute they got home it was, 'Those goddamn orphans broke my step again.' So it was a big facade."

A big facade—like the way other former Protestant orphanage residents repeatedly describe the public image that masked their reality.

A facade epitomized by visits from Ladies' Committee members or Children's Aid workers, he says—when everyone knew they were coming. "We were told, 'Okay, we've got to clean this; we've got to do this, we've got to do this,'" says Paul. "We knew someone big was coming."

And a facade maintained by the public face the staff put on for newspapers or TV stations or in fundraising letters.

"Whenever there was a picture taken in the orphanage, they would march everybody in and get them all dressed up with their little bow ties and their whatever," Paul remembers. "And then as soon as the photographer was gone, they'd beat your ass because you didn't have your tie on straight."

MAINTAINING THE IMAGE

Through the years, the orphanage's publicity committee actively sought good exposure, and that stretched into 1968, when Paul was still there, until the orphanage closed in 1970.

"We had a picture of our president and a brief item, in the *Mail-Star*, of our 1968 annual meeting, also an item about the many groups who entertained our children at Christmas and during the year," notes the 1968–69 publicity report.

"We are indebted to Mrs. J. E. Stanbury and the TV staff who so kindly consented to come to the home and make a tape of our superintendent, Miss Alley, and the children, at play and prepare a nice programme for the 'Kindness Club' on TV which was appreciated and enjoyed by all."

Other public reports play up the positive.

"Miss Fry the tutor feels the children are doing as well as can be expected, with their school work," it says, going on to report a range of outings–to the theatre; to a party at Saint Mary's University; to a restaurant and a hockey game, "where they were given each...new hockey sticks, and ball point pens.

"The Mothers Union St. John's Fairview [Parish] asked to come and make a tour of the home the evening of January 25, seventeen came, and all thought the home was so clean and cheerful looking."

THE KIND ONES

PAUL SAYS THE records will never show what really went on at the Halifax Protestant Orphans' home.

He encountered only occasional kindness. And like other former residents who can't name most of the matrons, the kind people are a different story.

He remembers Mrs. Hamilton—"a beautiful little lady"— whom others from that era also single out. One document lists her as one of the "housemothers," which may have been another way of saying "matron," since "Miss Gray"—Linda Gray-LeBlanc—is also listed as such. Some former residents remember Mrs. Hamilton helping in the kitchen.

But Linda, just eighteen and back at the orphanage as a matron, was his favourite. Linda, as documents show, took the children everywhere, from the Halifax Shopping Centre, to Expo 67 in Montreal—although Paul refused to go because that was a weekend with his "father" and he didn't want to miss time with "the most wonderful man that ever entered my life."

Paul loved Linda too.

"When I got there, she was the one person, if you stood fifty people in front of you, but you put a candle on one of them, they stood out," he says. "She had this aura about her where you could tell that there was a heart somewhere in there.

"The only thing that appeared good to me was Linda."

He developed a crush on the young woman. To impress her, he once organized an elaborate scheme to steal a small TV for her birthday. He brought it to the orphanage, and she told him to take it back–but she never told on him.

"I noticed, looking back at it, I was never punished when she was there. Because see, it's like being a prison guard; you got to earn your stripes with the rest of guards before they trust what they're going to let you see. If they're abusing the prisoners, they're going to slowly bring you into that. They're not just going to say, 'Okay, go over and kick the shit out of this guy.' It's like a union-type thing. You've got to join it and you've got to prove yourself.

"And where she was new,...I can remember her many a times being told, 'You're getting too close to the children,' or 'You can't show your feelings,' or whatever, because she'd have a little girl in her arms, rocking her or talking to her or whatever, and they'd say, 'No, no, you can't do that.'"

When he went to foster homes, kindness took on a different meaning.

"There was a couple of foster homes that were quite nice," he says. "The people treated me like I was a human being instead of a paycheque....They didn't hit you. That was the main thing....

"If you weren't beat, or if you weren't criticized...and they didn't treat you like a piece of garbage in the first half hour, you thought, 'Well, there's potential here.'"

But it never lasted.

Paul never felt loved–just a paycheck, a little over a hundred dollars a week for foster parents back then. He was savvy to their real motives, even then.

"Obviously they wouldn't be hitting me if they cared about

me, so you automatically know that they have no interest in you whatsoever. They're just looking for the money. In certain instances, you would have five or six kids all living in one foster home. The parents were geniuses because they'd get one at seven years old, one at eight years old, one at nine years old, one at ten. They'd buy the clothes and then pass them down, and meanwhile they're making all this [money].

"You knew exactly what was going on."

One home stands out for another reason.

When Paul arrived, the woman seemed nice. She welcomed him. She prepared a big meal. He hoped, like he'd hoped so many times before, that "this may be it."

Then his new foster father came home.

"He says, 'Oh my Jesus, not another bastard to look after.' So you're sitting there and you're thinking, 'Okay, I've been called a bastard and he hasn't even asked what my name is.'"

Things escalated from there.

"I'm not making any excuses whatsoever. I am the only one who is responsible for me," Paul says, before telling the story.

"Even when I was thirteen years old, I never asked anyone to take responsibility for what I did. But you know, you put a wall up, and just when you think that wall can come down, the father of the house comes in and says, 'Here's another bastard to look after.' And then you go in, you sit down, you're ready to eat, and every feeling in your body—it's like a whirlwind inside your head. You know, you're thinking of the orphanage...and you're confused.

"So I said, 'I realize you went through a lot of trouble for this; I really appreciate a nice home-cooked meal.' This is an hour and half after I got there, okay?...But I said, 'I'm really not hungry at this time; maybe I'll eat it later.'

"He gets up from the end of the table, puts the plate on his hand, grabs me by the back of the head, [breaks] the plate in my face....

"I ended up in a lot of trouble over that one," he says. "I retaliated quite strongly. I used a knife."

He doesn't want to say any more about that.

But he thinks of the last strands of hope he still had then: that someday, things might be different.

"I knew what I could give these foster parents: a kid that they wanted, that they could love, that they could be proud of. But I needed something in return. And before I got a chance to tell these people in the orphanage or in the foster homes what my plan was, they'd automatically put their plan [into motion], which put that wall up again, so I never did get the chance."

❧◦❧

LONGING FOR A HOME

DESPITE PAUL'S TOUGH exterior, "for survival," he poured out his hurt and his desperation in poems he kept to himself.

One of them, called "One Boy," encapsulates his life as a child. It speaks to his own desperation, and echoes the agony of so many orphanage children over so many years.

One boy no friends no family what does he do
He has learned to have no trust in you and you and you
The future is dark and filled with gloom
For when everyone is gone he is locked in a room...
One boy no friend no family to share
All he wants is for someone to be there
A gentle hand to embrace
But instead it's a fist to the face.

He wrote these and other lines when he was thirteen, still hoping to find a home.

"Paul is not suitable for any home," he read in one of his old case files many years later. But like most of the documents from his childhood, particularly from the orphanage, it didn't reveal the other side–the child's side.

"As a child, nobody would listen to you, to say, 'Why did you do this?' he says. "'How are you being treated here?' Not once, in all the years I'd been in foster homes, orphanages, and things like that, have I ever been questioned to say, 'How did these people treat you?'"

As time passed, the circumstances hardened Paul, who had built that "wall" years earlier; at the orphanage, he'd stand in the yard, sizing up the other kids, seeing who might "earn their way into my little circle."

"I had been brought up–you trust nobody, you don't trust your parents, you don't trust your teachers, your doctors, your police–nobody's allowed in my circle, and that's how you survive."

One Boy No Friends No Family Just Me
Sad And Lonely But No One Can See
No One To Love Him Where Will He Go

One Boy No Friends No Family All Alone
Feelings Are Blocked Only A Heart. Of Stone
The Future Is Dark And Cold
All He Wants Is Someone To Hold

One Boy No Friends No Family Anywhere
Sad And Lonely But No One To Care
The Days Pretend To Be Filled With Delight
But His Feelings Are Those Of Fright

One Boy No Friends No Family What Does He Do
He Has Learned To Have No Trust For You And You And You
The Future Is Dark And Filled With Gloom
For When Every One Is Gone He Is Locked In A Room

One Boy No Friend No Family To Share
All He Wants Is For Someone To Be There
A Gentle Hand To Embrace
But Instead Its A Fist To The Face

One Boy No Friends No Family No Life To Live
To Be Somebody Else There Is Nothing He Would Not Give
For His Mind Is Tired And His Heart Is Weak
All He Sees Is A Future Dark And Bleak

One Boy No Friends No Family Why Do They Do This
All He Needs Is A Warm Soft Kiss
The Others Were Not Treated Like Me
All He Needs Is A Chance And You Would See

One Boy No Friend No Famly I. Guess This Is It
More Beatings More Abuse More Of The Same Old Shit
Well Someday If I Am Still Here
The World Well Know This Boy Did Care
                    One Boy

Paul Sabarots wrote this poem on looseleaf paper when he was a child. *(Paul Sabarots)*

Back then, he'd plot his escape, thinking, "How am I getting out of here? Who am I taking with me?"

"I wanted to take every little kid who was there with me."

But he couldn't save them—or himself.

As a teenager, in and out of foster homes and group homes, Paul kept getting into trouble, looking at the world through wary eyes and sizing people up by looking into theirs—a student of the harsh side of human nature far too soon.

"Growing up on the streets, you study people; you tell by their eyes," he says.

"Children are a hundred times smarter than what we give them credit for, regardless of what child it is. They see things and they feel things that we can't even imagine as adults. So by going into a home and feeling rejected, like I said, you've put a wall up there. That wall—it's not made out of brick. It's made out of stainless steel, and it takes an awful lot for someone to get through."

By sixteen, even his own barriers couldn't help.

He was sniffing glue, using heroin, speed, acid, paint thinner—anything he could get. He was stealing, doing "a lot of break-and-enters" for the money.

He ended up in reform school—Shelburne School for Boys—for three months, he thinks, for the accumulation of his behavior.

The man he calls his father eventually took him in. "He would not give up on me," Paul says, "no matter how bad things got.

"I put him through hell because I was a drug addict. I was doing everything.

"It's a way to block out things—repress, I guess. Put aside," he says. "So you get into drugs, you get into drinking....You find a vice that will take the place of the hurt."

But a turning point came when Paul almost died.

He'd overdosed and police found him lying on a Halifax street around three o'clock in the morning.

"I had blood pouring out of me—my nose, my ears—puking blood....

"They [had] already done this three or four times before that, the police and the hospital," he says. "This last time, I was in there and I was lying on the bed...and I've got the tubes in me....The doctor comes in and my dad was there; he took my dad out, but they forgot to close the door, and I heard him telling my dad, 'If Paul doesn't stop what he's doing...he's going to be dead in three months....He is polluting his system with drugs....One of these times, he's either going to overdose, or he's just going to drop dead—period.'

"And it was the first time in my entire life that I saw my father crying."

Paul pauses for a few moments and his eyes, for the first time, appear to water.

"I looked at him and I realized at that point how much hurt I had caused him," he says. "When I saw him standing there crying, I thought, 'Oh my God, what have I done with my life?' and something just hit me like a bolt of lightning and I said to myself, 'That's it; I am never touching drugs again as long as I live.'"

He kept his promise and detoxed on his own—getting a friend to tie him to his bed so he wouldn't use.

The bad memories are harder to kick, even after years of success in the retail business, after working his way up on the oil rigs, installing cable, and then owning his own business as a private sheriff, where he removed kids from unsuitable foster homes, removed elderly people from abusive homes, and chased down kids who were behaving just like he had in the past.

He's tried to create the kind of life he never thought he'd have when he wrote that poem, and when he got that tattoo with the words "Mom" and "Dad" on his arm.

Paul only met his biological dad once, when he was sixteen and his mother called him to her home. She introduced her son to a man who couldn't speak English and told him: "That's your father." She said he wanted to take Paul home to live with him in Saint-Pierre and Miquelon. But Paul was bitter then, and refused to speak to the man who, he found out later, hadn't known for most of Paul's childhood that he even existed. He tried to reconnect decades later, realizing "the more you hold something in, the blacker it gets." But it didn't work out.

Today Paul Sabarots has a happy home and a family that loves him. *(Paul Sabarots)*

The man he'd always considered his father, the most wonderful man he'd ever known, died in the 1970s.

And he's had a long, difficult, complex, sporadic relationship with his mother. They've mostly been estranged. There are details he doesn't want to get into. It's still painful.

But today, he has his own home, and people who love him. His second wife, Trudy, "my favourite wife," he says with a laugh, has helped him trust just a little bit more.

"In seventeen years, we've never had an argument," he says, sitting on a dining room chair, his hand, with his wedding ring, touching the table. "She knows what family is about."

He has two daughters from his previous marriage; he's tried to shelter them from the sometimes-bleak ways of the world. One of them, worried that reliving the past might be too hard on her dad, calls several times as the frigid January afternoon wears on and the sun starts to set, illuminating his faded tattoo.

It sweeps across the ice on the lake that borders his backyard, and across the patio where he asked Trudy to be his wife.

It streams past the fire that warms his living room, near the cookies and coffee she's prepared for the day.

It rises up a wall of pictures in his hallway, crowned by a word that's also been a lifelong wish:

"Family."

Chapter Six: Number 11
James Underwood

JAMES UNDERWOOD ARRIVED in the dark. It was quiet as he walked through the door and up the stairs to the boys' dorm, where everyone else was asleep.

He was scared that first night in the orphanage.

He cried.

Georgina—a staff member he later called "Georgie Boy"—sat on his bed and rubbed his back, soothed him until he fell asleep in the place that would become his home for a year.

It was the latest in a series of homes in a "rough and tumble time" that began when James was six, after his parents split up and the unravelling of his family began.

James and his siblings moved from neighbourhood to neighbourhood with their father, an alcoholic who tried to raise them on his own. At one point, they ended up in "a tarpaper shack," and then in a home that had only an outhouse, until his father's drinking got worse and he collapsed and went to hospital with pneumonia.

James and his brothers and sisters stayed alone in the house for a week with no water and no power. Social Services came and sent the boys to foster homes and their sisters to St. Paul's Home for Girls.

And then, in 1967, they sent James—"a problem child"—to the orphanage.

He encountered some kindness—from "Georgie Boy" who was there for just a short time. And from Linda Gray-LeBlanc "with her glasses and pleated skirts." And from a matron named Langley (possibly Isabelle Langley, whom others remember reading them ghost stories) and from Mrs. Coffin and a "sweetheart" named Regina, who knew James liked prunes and gave him extra.

But he was afraid of the rest.

"The hair on the back of your neck [stood] up and you got a chill down your spine" when they walked by, he says.

Someone is going to get disciplined, he thought then.

James often watched the discipline, as did others, when the matrons hit the boys and girls with the wooden paddles other former residents have described.

It often happened in the dining hall, by the head table, where the matrons sat and doled out punishment when children argued or refused to eat or violated other orphanage rules.

"It was always like a public spectacle," he remembers. "They would be called up to the table and they would be chastised and they'd turn around and they'd get smacked with that....You got scared and felt bad for them."

James got the paddle once, too. On his behind. He isn't sure why.

"It hurt, and it was humiliating."

But these were familiar emotions even before the orphanage—where he was "Number 11"—the number on his toothbrush, the number on his locker, the number on his bed. The number on his boots, the number on his coat. The number of years since he had been born.

"Everything I owned, everything I was, was Number 11," he says. "I felt like a number."

But like some of the other former residents, James says the orphanage was better, in some ways, than his life afterwards.

At least, it was much better than being a foster child—a label he tried to hide, pretending his foster parents were his real parents, ashamed that they weren't.

"It was like a hidden identity. I would tell people I was living with Mom and Dad, but in the orphanage we were all on the same playing field; they were in the same situation I was," he says. "Everybody was the same. We were on equal footing then."

❧

BEFORE THE ORPHANAGE

JAMES HAD RARELY felt on equal footing with other kids, even when he'd lived at home, when he and his siblings were always the kids "on the other side of the track."

First, on Willow Street, his earliest memories—good memories, even though he got a dart in the leg once, and he once got hit by a car but wasn't seriously injured.

His parents were still together then. His father was a boilermaker at the Halifax dockyard. His mother stayed home with James, his two brothers, and his two sisters.

If his parents had problems, they hid them from their kids. They had good times.

James loved the police. He'd run away so they would catch him and take him to the station and give him candy. He laughs about it now, sitting in his living room with his wife, Judy, who still sees remnants of his past in the present.

"I always wanted to be a policeman," he says of those early days on Willow Street. "Back in those days, it was cops and robbers and shooting and getting the bad guy."

They had "good Christmases" there too. And he remembers that they "just played together" through the seasons.

But things took a turn when James was about six, after they'd moved to a subdivision in the Spryfield area of Halifax.

He still sees the moments in his memory and recalls the guilt that followed him for years afterward.

"I only ever remember one time of them really fighting," he

says. "That's when we were in Leiblin Park, before our family broke up.

"We went shopping, and it was towards the winter, I believe; it wasn't snow, but it was a real rainy day. We were shopping in downtown Halifax, back in the days when they had some of those department stores on Barrington Street. When we came back, I was sitting in the front between my mother and father and everybody else was in the back. What had happened is, my dad had got out because it was raining, and he went to open the door; we were all still in the car, but I remember I turned the car off–and because I did that, my mother slapped my hands.

"You can understand why. I mean, children shouldn't touch ignitions or controls of the car. Well, I was crying, and when my dad came back, he asked me why I was crying, and I said, 'Mom slapped me.' Him and my mother had a very bad fight that night, and I remember he kicked her out, and I remember her putting her hand through the door window.

"That was really the last time that my mother and father were actually together," he says. "I'd always blamed myself for their breakup because of that."

His mother moved to Halifax and took cleaning jobs. She visited a few times when their father was away.

Life for James and the rest of his family "started to spiral down."

"My dad was now trying to raise five kids, and sometimes his work would take him to Saint John and stuff like that. I remember one time; it was around Easter. Dad was coming back, and I believe he had been drunk, because he had [driven] the car off the road into the ditch, and apparently he had all of our Easter candy in the car. We were trying to find it, and we couldn't find it—someone else got it before we could get there."

His father's drinking had been a problem for as long as James could remember. He was an alcoholic, and the alcoholism worsened as the family's fortunes faded.

They moved from their "nice" house in Leiblin Park to a "tarpaper shack" on Margate Drive, in the Cowie Hill area of Halifax.

"Tarpaper shack, literally," James says. "There was just studs, and I can remember there was a loft and just tarpaper on the outside. There [were] no real finishings on the inside, but that's where we lived."

They slept on mattresses and stayed for about six months.

Then they moved to a one-bedroom house on Pine Grove Drive in Herring Cove. It didn't have a bathroom, so they used an outhouse. His father slept on a davenport in the living room. The kids shared a bedroom: the two girls in one bed, the three boys in the other.

"We didn't really have anything. We used to have very strict restrictions on food. My dad was a great cook and my dad was a great baker, but, you know, there was just not enough food."

James and his siblings were "all very close," but his sisters were the primary disciplinarians—harsh disciplinarians. They whipped the boys with frying pan cords.

In those days, parents or other guardians were "a lot more aggressive," he says.

"Just a fact of life, you know? We were taught things the hard way, through hard knocks."

In those days, he learned other things through example.

He saw a lot of things kids shouldn't see: drunken neighbours; fistfights inside and outside their home.

Around this time, when he was ten, James had already started drinking.

And smoking.

And stealing.

"I was a real thief. I could steal your eyes out of your head," he says.

"I'd smoke and steal [Dad's] cigarettes. When we were around all that alcohol, I used to steal my dad's beer. I was ten years old, and I drank eight pints of Ten Penny....I can remember the next day, dragging along the floor, vomiting as I went. I was so sick."

James stole from other people, too; from stores; even from the collection plate.

"I never did it because I wanted to be malicious and hurt people," he says. "It's just that we were without. I mean, we were so poor."

So poor he'd steal the thirty-eight cents needed to buy his own cigarettes, or scrounge the butts others left on the ground.

James calls himself "an old soul, because we had to grow up so early." But at night, he was a terrified little boy, sharing that small bedroom with his brothers and sisters, imagining monsters in the dark, thinking about death as he looked across Halifax Harbour from Herring Cove.

"From my window in the bedroom we could always look over on a clear night and we could see the fire from the [Imperial Oil] Refinery. [We] used to always be scared to death, because we were told that if that fire ever went out, we would all die. I don't know [who said it], but it was a fear I had. We were all going to die, because the world was going to burn up."

Then, one day in 1966, his world changed forever.

It was November. His father was no longer working.

James woke up and looked out the bedroom window. He saw his father lying on the ground.

"He [had] pneumonia and he tried to go to the washroom, and when he was on his way back, he fell and cut himself up. He was quite sick, so we rushed out and we got him back in."

An ambulance came and took him to hospital. By coincidence, that day the power company cut off the family's electricity, because his father hadn't paid the bill. They lost water too, because the pump wouldn't work.

For days, they walked to the fire station to get water in jugs. Neighbours may have given them a bit of food.

Then James came home from school at the end of the week "and the welfare was there."

 ⁓ ⊙ ⋆⁓

FOSTER HOMES

THE FOSTER HOMES that followed added to James's fears. These were strange people. Unkind. People that should never have been allowed to take in kids, he says. He doesn't want to name them.

His first foster home was in East Jeddore, where he lived with an elderly woman who had three children of her own and took in other foster kids.

"It was really a means of support for her and her family," he says—a familiar refrain among children from this and earlier decades.

He stayed for just a week.

One of her sons beat up James's little brother, so James "put a whooping on him."

"And then I took my little brother and we ran away. We were going back to Halifax; we were going to make it back home, but we didn't know where we were, so of course the police were sent for us, and I remember the police—the RCMP—picking us up and bringing us back."

They were on Highway 7 and they had walked for about two hours. When they returned to the foster home, James was defiant.

"Her son wore glasses, so I called him 'Goggle Eyes,'" he remembers.

"She said, 'What did you call my son?'

"I said, 'I called him Goggle Eyes.'

"Well, she slapped me across the face and called the welfare....They took my older brother and moved us, and left my younger brother there in East Jeddore."

James and his older brother moved to a home in West Jeddore. They could look across the bay and see where they had been—where their little brother still was. "We were worried about him. Would we ever be together again?"

James stayed in West Jeddore for about ten to twelve weeks. He was eleven, his older brother thirteen.

The foster father was a fisherman who was often away. The mother had two small children.

"She didn't know how to raise kids, plain and simple," James says.

"She would send us to school...and she would make us a lunch, and the only thing she put in our lunch was a half a sandwich," says James. "I can always remember being hungry."

They had no plumbing or running water. The bathroom, as in the tarpaper shack, and on Margate Drive, was an outhouse.

James's foster mother rarely interacted with him or his brother. But for the first time, his biological mother—whom they'd only seen "on the odd, odd, odd occasion" over five or six years—came to visit them in the foster home.

She took them out for a drive.

"This lady afterwards, when my mom was gone...she called my mother a whore because she was dating another man"—a man she would eventually marry, James remembers.

"She said that to me. So I said, 'Well, you're an old witch!' So I get slapped across the face and the welfare's called. But when the welfare came to get me, they couldn't take me, because I had just developed the mumps—so they had to keep me for a week or so."

After that, social workers drove James and his older brother to another foster home in Cooks Brook, a small community in Nova Scotia's Musquodoboit Valley. James thought they were both going to live there. But they dropped his brother off and took James—the "problem child"—to the orphanage, where he spent a year in the "very intimidating and regimental" institution that was, at that time, just three years away from closing.

A GLIMPSE OF LIFE IN 1967

James Underwood's story, like the stories of most children who lived at the orphanage in 1967, isn't told in the official orphanage documents, although the children's names occasionally appear in passing references.

As is typical in the documentation as far back as the 1800s, the documents offer only surface outlines and fleeting glimpses of reality–the periphery of lives that ran much deeper than reports of activities like trips to Big Cove Camp and Rainbow Haven Beach, to hockey games, to variety shows, to the circus, to parties, and to Expo 67.

Lives that ran much deeper than reports of gifts, Easter candy, and ice cream cones. Deeper than the minutiae of household repairs and purchases.

Staff, as always, received the "appreciation" of the Ladies' Committee in a year when five matrons or housekeepers left, including head matron Margaret Langley, who took a job at the Nova Scotia School for Boys in Shelburne.

"We are very pleased," the Ladies wrote in their 1967 annual report, "with the care and interest shown in the children."

But sometimes more troubling matters–and more essential truths–emerge, as they did in a report from new head matron Mary Dolphin about the mental health of children in the orphanage.

"There is a problem with one of our boys, I would like to discuss," she wrote in June 1967.

I think he is badly in need of psychiatric care, it would in my opinion help very much, he seems to have two characters, he is a sweet boy at times, and he can change so quickly.

He beat up a little boy from school the other day, and I'm afraid there is going to be trouble over that. Actually he is not a good influence on the other children. I think, however, it is worthwhile trying to help him, for if he is sent to Shelburne to the Boys' School, he will be completely ruined.

As a matter of fact, approximately fifty percent of our children should have psychiatric help, if only we could get a psychiatrist to donate some time for the children, the same as we have our medical doctor, donating his services.

Evolving research would show the treatment children endured in this and other institutions can cause great psychological harm—as many orphanage residents can attest.

STRUCTURE AND PREDICTABILITY

THE ORPHANAGE GAVE James more "structure" and more predictability than he'd had before.

It appears, from his and other former residents' recollections, that matrons were no longer routinely practicing the most severe forms of psychological punishment—like tying children to beds or putting them in closets.

But James still didn't want to be there.

He missed his family.

"I wanted to be back with my brothers and sisters and my parents," he says.

The impersonal institutional routines, and the stigma of being in an orphanage, resonate to this day. He hates food lines—"walking along with a plate, waiting to be served"—because it reminds him of his days as a number.

In the orphanage, bells rang for getting up and going to bed, and for breakfast, lunch, and dinner. Children lined up to get their meals, to take their baths, to brush their teeth.

"You'd get bathed, and...unless you were number one, you never got into a fresh bath of water," James says. He remembers hiding once, naked, in a locker, because he didn't want to get in the tub.

Other hygienic rituals were also out of the ordinary. The orphanage didn't have toothpaste. "You would get salt," James remembers.

"So you'd walk up, put your hand [out], and they had these little racks with 'Number 11' and all the toothbrushes. So you could take your toothbrush; they'd pour salt in your hand, you'd put that on your toothbrush, and you'd go and brush your teeth."

Outside the orphanage, he experienced the same kind of ostracism other former residents have described. When he was at home with his family, on "the other side of the tracks," kids teased him about his clothes—his father's clothes, three or four sizes too big, that James used to wear.

Now, when he was outside the orphanage, they teased him about where he lived, which was always obvious to outsiders.

"When it came time for school, you were lined up to get your rubbers on, you were lined up to go out the door, you were always kind of like in a group. I remember back then the kids in Mulgrave Park didn't like us orphan kids, so they'd throw snowballs at us, taunt us, and tease us. They called us 'the orphan kids' and all kinds of names and stuff."

But "the orphan kids" found ways to cope. They even had fun behind the walls—or the "fenced enclosures"—of the yard where they were expected to stay.

James organized a boys' club called The Hawks. He circles his fingers over his eyes and laughs, letting out a loud bird-like call that was their signal.

"We just kind of grouped together and we would have our meetings. We probably fixed the world," he says with a laugh.

"I remember we were going to join together and we were going to take down any of those bullies up in Mulgrave Park. We were going to fight together and protect one another, and all that kind of stuff."

꩜

EXPO 67

JAMES HAS OTHER "good memories" of the year he turned twelve. It was also the year Canada turned one hundred, an anniversary celebrated at Expo 67—and by the trip of a lifetime for the orphanage children, who went to Montreal with "Miss Gray and Mrs. Holloway as monitors," as one of that year's reports notes.

But the trip later haunted Miss Gray—Linda Gray-LeBlanc—for decades.

They were in Montreal. James and his friends were on a tramway headed for La Ronde, the amusement park that was part of the grand exhibition.

"We were transferred to another tram," he says. "They wanted more money and I said, 'No way!'" he recalls. "I'm thinking, 'I'm not going to have money to get on the rides,' so I said, 'No, we're not getting on; we'll walk.'

So James and a friend hopped off—and so began another frightening adventure for a boy whose childhood had already been full of so many twists and turns and troubles.

"I remember walking down the ramp thinking, 'I better rethink this.' We turned to go back, but the tram left," he says. "We took off in a run, and as long as we could see the tram we were okay, but I remember we came to a canal of water that cut us off—so then we were trying to find a bridge or something to get there. So the short of that was: we got lost, and once again the police had to find us."

The police found them and took them to an administrative office, where the boys spent the rest of the day.

They never did get on the rides.

And Linda—until James contacted her almost fifty years later—had always thought she was to blame; that she had lost track of the children under her care.

"Poor Linda," he says.

"You didn't lose those kids," he told her after he'd read her self-published memoir and tracked her down. "You were a very good escort;...a very good caretaker."

Other outings are just as memorable, although for different reasons.

Like other former residents, the draw of a parent was strong even for the children who had been given up to strangers. James cherished his dad's visits—especially an outing that was only the second time in his life they'd been alone together. The first time, when they'd lived at home, his father had taken him for an ice cream after his first dental appointment. "We're cold on the outside," his dad said of the rare treat. "We might as well be cold on the inside."

The second time, when James was living at the orphanage, his father took him to see a double feature.

"The first one was a scary [movie]; it messed my head up. But the second picture was John Wayne in *The War Wagon*, and John Wayne was always my hero," he says.

Years later, while attending college in Moncton, he told some friends about it. It was around the time of his birthday, so as a present, they gave James a copy of the movie—the story of a rancher who gets back at a corrupt businessman who has wronged him.

~⊚~

AFTER THE ORPHANAGE

JAMES LEFT THE orphanage—the place that felt like a prison—when he was twelve. But adults continued to wrong him.

He went from the orphanage to the foster family in Cooks Brook that had taken in his older brother, Charles. His foster parents were an older couple with grandchildren.

"It was wrong to put kids there," he says. "I look back at it and I say it was 'the haunted house on the hill.'"

The woman was "a kind lady," but the man was a "standoffish guy" who James describes as "stingy" and "verbally abusive." The man swore at them. He called them "welfare kids." He slapped them a few times.

"There would be no acts of kindness, really, to us," James says.

Even when his foster father took them to drive-in movies, they'd have to sneak in without paying.

When he drove them to the Co-op in Shubenacadie, they'd sit in the open back of his half-ton truck, even in winter. James says it felt like they'd "freeze to death."

The couple lived off their Old Age Security and the money the Province paid them to look after foster children. James believes money was their only motivation for being foster parents.

Even so, they lived in poverty.

"There would be many occasions that, literally, the food

cupboard would be bare," he recalls. "You had raisins and apples down in the pantry and that was it—what you ate for a week."

"If you look at those three foster homes, [by] today's standards as they should be, you would not put children in those homes at all," he says.

He sees that even more clearly now. James and his wife, Judy, have raised two foster kids of their own, and they say they went through stringent security checks that didn't seem to exist when James was a child.

"There were no case reviews. Not one time did social services ever come and do a case review with us, saying, 'How are you getting along? Are you getting enough to eat?' None of that. 'How are you treated?' No. So really we fended for ourselves."

James lived at the last foster home for almost four years; during that time, his mother had been working as a cleaner at Dalhousie University in Halifax and she had begun the process of trying to get her children back. She had a one-bedroom apartment on Jubilee Road. First, she took her two girls out of St. Paul's Home for Girls and got them jobs as cleaners at Dal.

She appealed to social services to reunite her youngest boy, still in East Jeddore, with his brothers in Cooks Brook. Charles, the oldest, at that time about seventeen, then joined his family on Jubilee Road. James and his little brother Cecil stayed behind in Cooks Brook for another year and a half. They wanted to be with their family and his mother "kept saying she was going to keep working on it."

"Eventually," James says, when he was fifteen, "we all got reunited."

The kids went to school during the day and cleaned with their mother—at her second job—at night.

They worked hard, saved their money. Eventually, she bought "a beautiful house."

James admires her for it.

"My mother knew nothing else but to clean floors; she was... not a professional lady by any means," says James. "And yet, because my mother worked hard, it was my mother that was able to bring us all back together."

When they were back together, he never talked to her about all the reasons they had been apart. Not even later, before she developed Alzheimer's disease and died. And he rarely talked about it with his brothers and sisters, whom he occasionally sees now at dinners Judy arranges, or on vacations.

"You know, I think when we were coming through all that, now coming together...I would say there were some key years of bonding that we didn't have."

⟡

CONFIDENCE AND PEACE

AT HIS FINAL foster home, James had spent as much time with his neighbours as he had with his brothers in "the haunted house on the hill."

The neighbours had kids his age. They played together, and he went to church with them on Sunday afternoons and evenings. It was then he realized what had been missing from his life—a "spiritual relationship" that changed everything.

"That is where I really gave my heart and my life to the Lord and became very involved with the Pentecostal Assembly," he says.

Prayer, James says, gave him "security" and "confidence" and "peace"—and he learned something he hadn't experienced as a child. "We show our love to God best in our love and appreciation for one another."

James eventually became a Pentecostal minister and helped raise money to build a church in Dartmouth, where he was the pastor for many years.

Before and after, like his mother, he worked hard for everything he got. He cleaned. He ordered supplies for a construction company. He dug ditches for five dollars an hour. He worked as a mail handler and a postal clerk and a management officer at Canada Post, where he kept rising through the administrative ranks.

But the past followed him. His faith had made him more confident, but he still doubted—not the Lord, but himself.

"All my life," he says. "All my life."

When he worked at Canada Post, which he did for thirty-five years, he received numerous promotions. But he only applied for one of those, he says, "because I didn't think I could do it."

His bosses saw something else. They called him tenacious: "Like a dog with a bone." They saw a work ethic born of struggle and survival. They saw the fierce fighting spirit he had brought to his other jobs, and to his time as a teenaged wrestler—"the Musquodoboit Mauler"—when he'd take on the "big guys" and lock his arms around them and—"like a leech"—not let go.

But Judy says that despite his ample accomplishments, she still sees the stain of her husband's childhood.

James Underwood calls himself "an old soul" because he had to grow up so fast. He and his wife, Judy, have raised two foster kids of their own. *(Author photo)*

"He's so bold and tenacious, and he's so strong in what he tries to do and tries to accomplish," she says, as her husband of almost forty-five years falls silent.

"And yet I still see how what happened in his young life has affected him—sometimes feeling insecure, sometimes feeling maybe unaccepted, or not as good as others."

She says it makes her feel bad to think that anyone would treat children, especially such vulnerable children, the way they did her husband and others.

"Was there nobody to show any love and concern?" Judy wonders. "Was there nobody with a little kindness in their heart? With a little compassion? With a little understanding?

"Didn't anybody even think to love them—or at least be kind?"

Chapter Seven:
Redemption
Elaine McLellan

ELAINE MCLELLAN WANTED to keep her family together.

But to do that, she had to break it apart, placing her children in the orphanage, crying "every day" they were there.

"Nobody would help me," she says, of those desperate days in 1968 after she left her alcoholic husband and had no money and no place to live.

Her family—and her husband's family—refused to take them in.

That was a long time ago, but the roots of her decision go back even further—to her own childhood and to what happened before she was even born.

To a war, and the shrapnel in her father's skull.

To poverty, and the cruelty in her mother's fists.

To a generational cycle of circumstances—alcoholism, violence, deprivation—that shaped the lives of so many of the orphanage children through the years.

Her father's picture hangs above her now as she sits on a sofa in her Halifax apartment with her daughter, Joan Wilson. Images of others, alive and dead, sit on tables, in photo albums, on a standing gallery by a window that looks out to the water. Her dad is wearing a military uniform. A poppy is pinned to the frame.

His voice is in her head.

"You goddamned Germans, I'm going to kill you!" he'd scream when he took his "spells" or came home drunk.

He had been wounded in the Second World War, after a soldier next to him was "blown to bits," and pieces of shrapnel had lodged in his head.

Elaine was four when her father came home. He was never quite right.

A photo of Elaine McLellan's father, war veteran William Canary, hangs in McLellan's home today. *(Author photo)*

"He had eight silver clips in his head from the war," she says. "He would take "spells," as they called it. He would just pass out.... We used to hear a lot of his war stories, and he drank quite a bit....[We lived] on Brunswick Street, I think, and I'd see him coming up the street. I knew he was drinking, and I'd run in the house and hide, because he'd go back

Elaine McLellan as a child, with her oldest sister, Ann. *(Elaine McLellan)*

to the war when he was drinking, and you were a German [to him] and he'd swing at you. I was too scared....

"He'd go after Mom, mostly, and she'd calm him down, and then she would put him to bed, and that would be the end of it," says Elaine.

"But I always ran and hid when I [saw] him coming, because I didn't want to be around him when he was drinking."

But Elaine loved him anyway.

They were "good friends," she says. "I guess because every time Mom would fight with me, he'd tell her to leave me alone."

Her father never struck her, but her mother often did—she slapped her in the head and in the face. Sometimes, she hit her with a broomstick.

"My mother beat me every time I turned around," she says. "For whatever reason. If she got mad at [my oldest sister] Ann, she'd beat me for it. You know, it just went on. I was going to leave home when I was eighteen and she said, 'If you leave home, I'll get the Mounties to bring you back,' and I thought that was true, so that didn't happen."

But Elaine found another way out.

She met a man while she worked at Maritime Paper making boxes. She married him at twenty. She didn't know then that he had a drinking problem.

Her oldest son, John, was just a baby the first time her husband came home drunk. It wouldn't be the last.

"He'd bring people home. 'This is my pal!' He didn't even know who they were, and then he's into the fridge and he's digging food out and cooking it for them. And then I called his mother and I told her he was drinking and [she said], 'Oh no; not again.'

"'Not again?' Apparently he stopped drinking for four years before I met him and then he started again."

⁂

HER DAUGHTER'S MEMORIES

ELAINE'S DAUGHTER JOAN, sitting beside her now, has only scattered memories of her father from back then—but she remembers his drinking.

"Dad drank my whole life," she says.

But she remembers his gentleness too.

She still smiles, thinking of the man who was quiet when he was sober and lively when he was drunk—a good man who always loved her mother, but who couldn't conquer an addiction that she, too, would battle later in her own life.

"The memories I have of Dad when I was young [are that] my father was such a quiet man. He was a very quiet man."

But only, mother and daughter agree, "when he wasn't drinking."

"And then when he drank, it was almost funny because— you're just a kid, right? Because he became so different. Not that he was ever an angry man or anything like that. I used to find Dad funny."

"He was funny," Elaine says. "He'd sing these dirty old songs."

But the disease wasn't funny, and eventually his alcoholism consumed everything.

He drank everything, even pure vanilla. He'd get "drunk sick" after binges that lasted a month, "and he'd see things and hear things," Elaine says.

When he stopped, he shook through withdrawal—got the DTs—and Elaine took him to detox. She took him again and again, even after she had packed all her belongings in garbage bags and gathered her kids together and got a ride to Halifax and stayed with her cousin at a military base for a week.

They had already moved many times and were living in the country near Noel in Nova Scotia's Hants County. He had spent most of the family's money on alcohol. Elaine was on welfare.

She had stayed with him for ten years—until she couldn't take it anymore.

"I heard for years, 'I'm going to stop, I'm going to stop, I'm going to stop,' and I'd go, 'Okay, then,'" she says. "And after ten years, it's like, 'No, he's going to keep telling me this.'"

So Elaine started phoning strangers–people whose names she knew only because her husband had mentioned them.

"I said, 'I'm leaving my husband and I need a drive to Halifax,' and nobody would take me. So then the school phoned me: 'Why aren't your children in school?'

"I said, 'Because I'm leaving my husband and I got to get the kids back to Halifax.'"

The school principal agreed to drive her.

"I packed all their stuff in garbage bags–all their clothing– and took them. I went to my cousin's place."

Her cousin couldn't keep them for long. She was living in military housing in Dartmouth's Wallace Heights, and she was afraid they'd get caught, so Elaine called Child Welfare and a social worker tried to help her find an apartment.

But the apartments were all too small for her and her children–Joan, John, Stephen, Danny, and Melvin.

"My father's side, and Mom's side–nobody would take us unless they separated us," Joan says.

"I asked my mother and I asked my sisters, and they didn't want any part of it," Elaine remembers. "'These are your children,' you know? They wouldn't take them. So I wrote a letter to his mother and father and I said, 'It wasn't my fault that your son's a drunk and he can't look after his children.'

"Nobody would help me."

Then Child Welfare started talking about separating the children–something Elaine had been trying to prevent all along.

A photo in Elaine McLellan's home of four of her six children: Joan (right), Stephen (front), Danny (left) and John (centre, back). Melvin, her youngest from her first marriage, and Philip, her son from her second marriage, are not pictured. *(Author photo)*

"You can't do that," she told them. "No. My kids aren't going to lose me and their father too. They won't know what's going on. They've got to have somebody."

"So they said, 'The Halifax Protestant Orphanage.' And I thought, 'Well, okay; they'll all be together, anyway.' I didn't know it was the way it was."

The way it was isn't fully told in monthly Ladies' Committee reports from that year—reports which paint glowing pictures of the orphanage's routines and its staff.

Joan, like many others, remembers it differently.

"They were mean," she says of the matrons—although she recalls a few exceptions.

And she missed her mother, who longed to be reunited with all of her kids.

"I cried every day the kids were in the orphanage," Elaine says, "because I'd talk to Joan and she'd be crying, and it was like, 'Oh my God, I've got to get my kids out of there.'"

Joan was eight when she went in with her brothers. She doesn't remember her first day; a social worker took them there. Elaine says she didn't have the heart to do it herself.

"At first I thought it was good, because they were going to be together—they weren't going to be separated," says Elaine. "I figured I'd get a place right away."

But Joan stayed for nine months—the younger children got out a little earlier—as her mother kept searching for a place where they could all live together.

Joan remembers a strict, unloving environment, punctuated by a few acts of kindness—from Mrs. Hamilton, who seemed to feel sorry for them and at least tried to be gentle as she enforced the rules—and from a matron named Mrs. Gomez and a woman who used to tell the children ghost stories—what Joan calls "Friday night fun."

But fun was rare.

Most matrons enforced discipline and order with an iron will and little sympathy. They rarely smiled, she says, or spoke a kind word.

Joan doesn't remember bed restraints, like the ones matrons had used in previous years. And while some residents from the 1960s recall corporal punishment, she says no one ever hit her, either.

She's grateful, she says, she didn't live there in earlier times. But she was still traumatized—"mentally abused."

Mealtime was an ordeal. They forced her to choke down food—like mashed tomatoes, bread, or turnips—she despised. If she didn't comply, they made her stay at the table all night long.

"I'd fall asleep at the table," Joan says. "I remember waking up in the morning and then it's breakfast time. They'd take your plate away."

She started hiding her food in napkins and sneaking it into the garbage to avoid punishment.

But what hurt more was watching the way they treated others, like her little brother Danny, who was only six. They'd send him to a "punishment room" for the entire day, she says. They'd make him stay at the dinner table when he wouldn't eat.

Elaine came to visit once and saw him lying by his plate with his head on the table. He looked like he had been asleep. He sat up and started to cry.

"It was dark in the room and I said, 'What's he doing in there? And they said, 'Well he's going to eat his supper.' And I said, 'What the hell is this?'

"...I looked at it, and it was like slop. I said, 'He's not going to eat that, and if you don't get him out of here, I'm going to take him out.'"

But they threatened to call the police and Elaine knew she had to stop arguing. She had no other place to take them.

"It's just that I needed a place to live."

Joan was helpless too. She couldn't protect her younger brother or others in the orphanage. It still hurts her to picture Danny washing out his own sheets when he wet his bed, or thinking about how the matrons wouldn't let him to go trick-or-treating because of it.

Or thinking about how they treated other children she didn't really know.

They'd yell at a little boy who had "something wrong with him mentally," she recalls. "They picked on him a lot, the people in the orphanage. They were very mean to him, just the way they handled him. I remember them grabbing him, pulling him by his arm. If he cried, they would put him up [in] the dorm."

Her brother Melvin, just four years old, cried sometimes, too. Back then, Joan told Elaine the matrons had made him cry, but she doesn't know why.

No two people were closer, Joan says, "from the time I started protecting him in the orphanage."

Back then, she says, "he was a good little guy—happy-go-lucky.

"Because he was four, he didn't have the whole understanding of not having Mom and Dad, because he always had me. He would wait for me to come home from school. He was always happy to see me when I came in from school, and when I left in the morning I remember telling him, 'I have to go to school, and someday you're going to be a big boy and go to school too, but right now, I have to go,...so wait for me. I'll be back after school; you wait for me.'

"He'd say, 'I wait for you all day.'"

But Joan was only eight. Her days in the orphanage and at school wore her down. All she wanted was to go home.

"They treated us like we had no parents," she says of the matrons. "We were orphans. They treated us like orphans."

So did kids who weren't in the orphanage—a stigma that remained through the decades.

"I remember kids walking by when we were out in the yard, which was rare. Even though we had a playground in the yard, I don't recall being out there much," says Joan. "The kids would walk by the fence and just make fun of you. 'Orphans!' and 'You're scruffy!' and just mean things, you know?

"They even knew in school, the kids in school knew where you came from, because...the clothing was whatever they got for donation, so like, nothing matched—just whatever they gave you to put on."

This seems to have been the case earlier as well. A March 1957 Ladies Committee visitors' report notes how "perfect" children looked during a buffet dinner and tour hosted at the home for the local Children's Aid Society—but not at other times.

"The smaller children could be better dressed," the report says. "Their overalls or play pants are usually falling down, either because they are too big, or buttons are missing, or they need suspenders. On the night of the party they all looked perfect, but at other times they are for the most part bedraggled."

"Bedraggled" is how outsiders saw them too. And how outsiders tried to make them feel.

And as the months passed, Joan and her mother felt like their lives were spinning more and more out of control.

"I remember talking to Mom and crying all the time and asking her every time she called–'Have we got a place yet? Have we got a place yet?'" Joan recalls.

Elaine was desperate to find a place. The orphanage wasn't what she had expected. She argued often with staff about their rules and their disciplinary practices. She wasn't even allowed to visit Joan on her birthday because it didn't fall on visiting day, which was only every second Saturday.

But she was at their mercy, like Joan and the four boys, who kept waiting to go home while facing the most basic of humiliations in the place where "there was always fear that you were going to get into trouble."

Joan remembers sitting all day on her bed in the dorm as punishment, and having to pee. "You weren't allowed off your bed to go ask to use the washroom, so you had to yell: 'I need to go pee!' They'd just ignore you."

One day, she was sitting in school. She raised her hand and asked to go to the bathroom. The teacher told her to wait until another student came back. She had become used to obeying what adults told her to do.

"I must have got distracted and I didn't see him come back, and because my teacher already said that, I didn't re-ask. I was just watching the door, waiting for this kid to come back, and of course couldn't hold it any longer....

"I was so embarrassed," she says. "You could hear it hitting the floor because I was sitting at my desk....

"So embarrassed."

Her teacher gave her a letter to take back to the head matron and told her not to open the envelope.

"I had a feeling of what they were sending home—that they were going to tell them I peed my pants in school and I [was] going to get in trouble.

"I tore it up. I tore it up and threw it away so they never knew what happened to me that day, because I didn't want the punishment. I didn't want to have to go and sit on my bed all day because I peed my pants in school."

Joan doesn't remember whether she and her brothers had all wet their beds in the orphanage, but they all wet their beds when they finally went home—a sign, she believes, of trauma.

"Five wet beds every day," Elaine says. "And the boys wet on their pillows.

"Oh God, it was awful."

∼❀∽

MELVIN'S DEMONS

THEY DON'T KNOW whether trauma from the orphanage had anything to do with what happened to Joan's youngest brother when he came home.

Melvin had been Joan's childhood "buddy." As he grew older, he started shoplifting and breaking into houses; he kept skipping school and running away. And as the years passed, he appeared in court constantly. He became addicted to opiates.

Eventually, he took his own life.

"I'd say to him, 'Melvin, talk to me; what's the matter?' Elaine remembers. "But he would say, 'Nothing's the matter.'"

She remembers one of the last times she saw him. "He was here one day to visit me, and one of the women that lives here fell outside; he was coming in and he stopped to help her; he got a blanket to put around her."

But his family could never seem to comfort him.

"He had demons. He had demons but nobody knows," says Joan.

❦

JOAN'S DEMONS

JOAN HAD DEMONS of her own.

Awful things were happening to her at home. She says she was sexually abused for years by her mother's second husband, now dead. Elaine—married four times to the "wrong fellas"— didn't know about it until years later. She was horrified, and she encouraged Joan to go to the police. Joan filed a report, but the man died of a heart attack before he could be found or charged.

"She was kind of devastated," Elaine says, "because she didn't think that was a punishment. But I told her—I said, 'Joan, that's a punishment. He was taken off of this earth not to bother anybody else.'"

The abuse, which Joan says started when she was eleven, bothered her for years. "It will be with me until I die," she says.

It's one of the reasons she started drinking—continuing a pattern of alcoholism that had followed her family for generations.

"I drank a lot," Joan says. She continued drinking, even after she had her two daughters and Elaine tried to get her into Alcoholics Anonymous. Her mom practically raised Joan's children while Joan held a job as a cafeteria worker.

"I worked and I drank," she says. "That was my life."

But she eventually got sober—and stayed sober. She's now raising one of her own grandchildren, and she's determined to give her the kind of childhood she and her mother didn't have.

"She's my redemption," Joan says.

"It's my turn to do it right. I didn't get it right the first time. Let's get it right the second time."

❦

FOR THE GOOD OF THE FAMILY

JOAN'S MOTHER TRIED to get it right too, but circumstances and family history got in the way. Still, Elaine's guilt over placing her children in the orphanage remains.

"Mom's felt guilty a long time," says Joan.

But "it was just life," she says. Joan, like her older brother John, often reminds Elaine she did her best.

"We used to have to tell her—'Mom, don't ever feel bad about the decision you had to make.'"

"But I still feel bad," Elaine says.

John, on the phone from his home in Ontario, says he doesn't remember ever being mistreated at the orphanage. He ran away once, but he has no idea why. He went back there once as an adult, and few memories stirred.

But he understands the struggles and the choices both parents–his dad, who had "a disease"; his mom, who faced its consequences–had to make.

"I wasn't a good mother," John remembers Elaine telling them.

"And we told her, 'Mom, you did what you had to do for the good of the family,'" he says. "So the biggest part that I can take away from this is just that she kept us together as a family group, and we are a close family....You can't say much more than that for a mom trying to take care of her kids."

"It was just life," Joan had said earlier.

And "life goes on," John says now.

But every now and then Joan–"a survivor"–thinks about the little girl she once was, before she learned "life can toughen you."

She sees glimpses of the innocence and the excitement of her childhood–fleeting memories, wrapped up in mystery and in pain. For a moment, she's back inside the orphanage, in "a room bigger than a closet...filled to the brim with brand-new toys."

"You can pick out anything you want," the matron told her, "because it's your birthday."

"I remember picking out this little pink case; it was only about this big," Joan says, holding out her hand, sitting by her mother, going back to the past.

"It had a little doll in it, and I think a little carriage for the doll–probably something like you'd see at the Dollar Store now," she says. "I thought it was so cute, and whoever my worker was at the time said to me, 'Oh, that's only one; why don't you pick out something else?'

"And I picked out the exact same thing, but in a blue case, and she said, 'Now there you go—you've got two dolls that can play with each other.'

"But I don't remember playing with them," she says. "Where did they go?"

Soon she's back in the present, sitting by pictures from the past. She stands and picks up photographs of her granddaughter—the "perfect little girl" she's trying to protect. The little girl is wearing a sparkly red bodysuit and ballet slippers, and she's smiling.

In other frames scattered around Elaine's apartment, little Joan, the child, smiles. Her cheekbones are high. Her hair is curled. She looks happy.

In an even older picture, her mother, just a toddler—in a blue dress and a matching bow—looks up, as though puzzled by what she sees.

And above her, her father—young then, in his military uniform—a poppy by his side.

Chapter Eight:
"I Want My Story Told"
"Margaret"

SOME WOUNDS NEVER HEAL, no matter how distant the pain.

She was almost ninety when we spoke over the phone from her Ontario home. It had been eighty-five years since she'd first walked through the doors of the Halifax Protestant Orphans' Home.

But it seemed like yesterday.

She wept as she told me my call had been an answer to her prayers, and like a pill for her pain.

"It's killed me for years," she said. "I want my story told."

She told part of it. But, despite my repeated attempts to reach her later, we never spoke of it again.

Perhaps she had changed her mind.

Perhaps the pain was still too raw, too deep, to talk about it anymore.

I don't know, so her name will remain private—we'll call her Margaret—and part of her story will become public because of the rare insight she provides as one of the oldest living survivors of the orphanage—and as a woman who may never see a reckoning.

The provincial government doesn't want to talk about what happened to her or the others, despite their painful memories, and despite the countless documents which show that its predecessors funded and sent children to the orphanage for decades while—former residents say—failing to protect them.

Margaret lived at the orphanage in the mid-1930s and early 1940s, when a woman named Edna Crook was head matron.

She remembers a "Miss Crooks" as "a terrible woman," who she says relentlessly strapped her and her little brother; who gave them "terrible beatings" that have haunted her for her entire life.

1940.

GOVERNORS.

W. McT. Orr, Esq., *President.*
N. C. Mitchell, Esq., *Vice-President.*
Walter Mitchell, Esq., *Treasurer.*
Rev. G. M. Ambrose, *Secretary.*

J. W. Brookfield, Esq.   F. E. Barnstead, Esq.
Rev. D. M. Grant.   G. H. Morrison, Esq.
F. Adams, Esq.   J. W. Gordon, Esq.
H. M. Stairs, Esq.

LADIES' COMMITTEE.

Mrs. E. D. Adams, *Honorary President.*
Mrs. Harold Oxley, *President.*
Mrs. G. E. E. Nichols, *1st Vice-President.*
Mrs. C. W. Stairs, *2nd Vice-President.*
Mrs. M. L. Boswell, *Treasurer.*
Miss Gwladys Woodbury, *Corresponding Secretary.*
Miss Mary King, *Recording Secretary.*

Mrs. G. M. Ambrose   Mrs. R. E. Inglis
Mrs. Walter Mitchell   Mrs. A. N. Jones
Mrs. H. C. W. Powell.   Mrs. H. S. Crosby
Mrs. W. A. Curry   Mrs. VanBuskirk.
Mrs. A. S. Carten   Mrs. H. W. Cunningham.
Mrs. C. Stayner.

MATRON.

Miss Edna Crook.

MEDICAL ADVISERS.

Dr. Evatt Mathers.   Dr. N. B. Coward
                            Dr. Doull.

This annual report from 1940 shows that Miss Edna Crook was the matron of the home at that time. *(Nova Scotia Archives)*

THE CHECKLIST

During the early part of the twentieth century, the Nova Scotia government required facilities it funded to fill out checklist-style surveys, asking orphanages about everything from the number of tablecloths they used to whether or not they disciplined children. Edna Crook always answered "no" when asked if children were subjected to "corporal punishment" or "solitary confinement." (See more in Afterword, page 211). It isn't clear if Edna Crook is still alive. If so, she would be a very old woman.

Margaret went into the orphanage when she was a little girl—around 1934 or 1935, when she was five. She isn't sure why, but she thinks her parents' separation may have been to blame—a common refrain among former residents through the decades.

Initially, she stayed for at least a year, when she was taken in by foster parents. She lived with them for four years, but her foster mother had "crippling arthritis" and had to send her back.

"The lady wrote me a letter...where she apologized for sending me back to the orphanage," Margaret recalled. "They wanted to take me back, but she was too sick."

So she remained in the orphanage until she was twelve.

Her maiden name appears in orphanage records from 1936, when the institution housed an on-site school, "under the supervision of Halifax School Board," according to its 1935 annual report—a slight document, and one of only a few remaining from that era. Older children went to Richmond School.

"The Home and the [in-house] School are visited each week by two members of the Committee in turn," the report says, without revealing what conditions they found, but taking the time to thank the matrons "for their capable and faithful care of the children of the Home"—a stark contrast to at least one little girl's reality.

"If you smiled and you shouldn't have, you got a damn smack for it," Margaret remembers.

So did her little brother.

"I wouldn't know what was wrong with him, but the poor little thing, he couldn't control his urine and he got beaten so bad," she says. "His nose was always running; his eyes were always running; he was a sick little boy and he used to cry because he peed himself, and they'd give him an awful beating and you'd hear him crying."

She cries now too. And apologizes for it. But continues.

"I need to get this out of my system," she says. "I need to do this, Dear. You know when you're sick and you can't vomit? Excuse me. That's what I need to do."

She's had anxiety for years, and sometimes, at its worst, it overflows. "I do a lot of crying," she says.

"I feel sorry for myself, and I don't want to feel like that because...I don't want to be a crybaby. I want to be very strong. People think I'm strong; people that know me—more of a leader than a crybaby....

"I got lots of beatings for crying, Dear."

And she got a lot of beatings for just about everything else. Many of Margaret's memories echo those of others who came later—children who couldn't even go to the bathroom without permission.

"We were not allowed to get out of bed at night, so of course we peed our beds," she recalled.

"We got a beating for that. If we were caught getting up to go to the bathroom, we got a beating. They were so cruel....

"They didn't have anybody that was kind. They were not allowed to be kind. They were fired—I'm pretty sure, they were fired if they were [kind]."

Instead, the matrons were cruel, emotionally and physically—sometimes humiliatingly so, like the time when Margaret was nearly twelve and had her first period.

"I was in school and there was a boy behind me," she says. "He put his hand up and he told the teacher that [my] bum was bleeding; I never knew anything about menstruation or anything—we were not told anything—so when I got home [to the orphanage], I got a beating for making my clothes dirty."

"Those memories—I'll never forget, Dear."

ACCOUNTABILITY

The provincial government has consistently refused to discuss the past or its predecessors' role in funding or sending children to the orphanage.

Or to address the lack of provincial supervision.

Or to answer Shirley Carter's request that it publically acknowledge and publicly apologize for past wrongs.

It has denied or ignored requests for interviews with successive community services ministers or the premier.

Instead, its public relations staff have issued brief, general, written statements, including one on behalf of former community services minister, Joanne Bernard.

"All children should live safe from harm and abuse," the statement says. "It's tragic to hear from people whose experience was different. We are searching our archival records to determine what involvement, if any, we had in the oversight, administration, and operation of this home during its operation."

In response to a 2017 Freedom of Information application I made in the process of researching this book—requesting all financial records, government documents, correspondence, or emails related to the orphanage—the department said it didn't have the documents.

"After a file search, we have located no records responsive to your application," says the letter from Aimee Standen, Manager, Information Services and Privacy. "Therefore, it is my understanding, pursuant to clause 7(2)(b) of the Act, that the Community Services does not have custody or control of the record(s) which would respond to your application."

Current Community Services Minister Kelly Regan did not respond to my 2018 requests for an interview.

"I hope someday they will apologize," says Shirley Carter, who lived at the orphanage in the 1940s. But she thinks she knows why they won't.

"They're afraid that they'd be liable and then [we'd] want money, which I wouldn't take," she says. "I have money. If I was broke, I wouldn't take a penny from them. Not a penny."

None of the residents who've told their stories have said they want financial compensation. In fact, some have stressed that money is not their motivation for sharing childhood experiences that have lasted a lifetime.

It is more a release of long-silenced voices.

Or, as Margaret put it, "a pill for the pain."

Chapter Nine:
A Safe Place
Veith House

THE STAIRS AT Veith House creak. They're "sanded," as Gail Gardiner puts it, "by one hundred years of little feet."

"I often think about that as I walk up and down the stairs," she says. "I always feel it."

As executive director of Veith House, she's heard the outlines of what happened here when the building was an orphanage, but she still hopes "there was some laughter and some joy."

⤜◎⤛

A SAFE SPACE

GARDINER SEES BOTH laughter and joy these days when other little feet touch the steps of the almost–century-old building–children stopping in for breakfast bags or to use computers or to hang out in a "safe space" with their friends.

The stairs in the front hall at the former Orphans' Home–now Veith House–are worn by "one hundred years of little feet." *(Author photo)*

A lot has changed–in the world and in the building–since Shirley Carter and Linda Gray-LeBlanc and other former residents lived here.

And since all the unknown children of centuries past–the "little waifs" and "wanderers" and "orphans" and "half-orphans" mentioned, but not named, in old orphanage documents–lived in the orphanage, too.

On this day in May 2018, neighbourhood men and women sip coffee and chat and laugh in what used to be the isolation room as Gardiner sits next door in a memorial room–a room created for former orphanage residents who come back–surrounded by old black and white photos and documents and orphanage ledgers. And surrounded by memories as enduring as the checkered black-and-white tile in the hallway, the old porcelain sinks in the bathrooms, the wooden planks on the stairs.

Veith House staff originally decorated a memorial room upstairs, but most of the orphanage children are senior citizens now, and getting up there isn't always easy. For some, the visits aren't easy either, but they're a necessary rite of passage—a remembrance and a testament to another time.

Staff made a concerted effort to acknowledge the past a few years ago after the emotional return of an unexpected visitor. Administrator Monica Marsh had been sitting in her office near the front door when an elderly woman came in. The woman fell to her knees and sobbed. She told Marsh a little about the abuse she had endured there all those years ago.

Marsh tried to track her down later and could never find her. But the visit gave her the idea for the room—a peaceful place in a now "happy place" that might help former residents heal.

As time passed, others returned as well.

Volunteer Aron Spidle started talking to them and writing down some of their memories. Those are now collected in a memorial book that sits on a table in a room dedicated to the past, as Gardiner reflects on the present and the future.

Veith House maintains a memorial room from its time as the Halifax Protestant Orphans' Home. *(Author photo)*

Former orphanage resident Linda Gray-LeBlanc sits in the memorial room at Veith House. *(Author photo)*

COMMUNITY HUB

REMEMBERING THE PAST is just a small part of what happens at Veith House these days, in this "community hub" that helps both children and adults who are often facing everything from financial struggles to mental health challenges to isolation, loneliness, and more.

The non-profit community centre has been providing variations of these services since it opened in 1970. Its mission from the beginning has been to help primarily low-income families in the north end of Halifax.

The range of services offered today are ever-evolving, depending on the need. For instance, Veith House's "apple kids," as Gardiner calls them, are children who come regularly for bags of breakfast food on their way to school. That program began by happenstance a few years ago when a couple of children showed up at the door on a January morning and told her, "We're hungry."

She didn't have any food at that time, but told them to come back after school.

"Ten showed up," she says, "so I ran downstairs. We had a bag of apples and I gave them all a bag, and...the next day more showed up, and more showed up. We now have upwards of forty-five children coming."

They receive nutritious snacks like juice packs or cheese or breakfast bars. But the name "apple kids" has stuck, even though the program has widened even further.

"They like being called the apple kids," Gardiner says.

As the kids came, they started hanging out in the building—initially fighting over the one computer in the coffee room, Gardiner recalls with a laugh. So staff gave them access to more computers and put them in "a giant room upstairs," which they now use after school.

"They can come and they can go as they want," she says of the children, who range in age from five years old to preteen. "These are kids who primarily live in Mulgrave Park, which is public housing, so we view it as a safe space—as a low-barrier program where the children can come and go. It's a safe space where they can socialize with their friends."

And they can feel at home—unlike the children who had been labelled "bedraggled" and "scruffy" and "orphans" and other derogatory terms in the past.

"It's just fun....The kids can be with their friends after school," she says, explaining that some may not be able to bring their friends home.

"It's just a hopping room. Like, I mean, from three to four [o'clock] our [office] computers don't work because they hog all our internet. We just do it with a sense of humour, and we do it because we just feel it's important with these kids.

"We always say, 'We weren't seeking out this program; they chose us.' And that's how we frame it. And if a kid has an off day, we just say, 'You need to go home today. Think about it and you're welcome back tomorrow.' We don't raise the problem again."

If a child has problems, they're encouraged to share them—unlike the suppression the former orphanage residents experienced.

Sometimes the apple kids share them by talking. Sometimes they share them through art—an art therapy program where they can draw or paint their feelings. And sometimes they write down what's happening in their lives and how they feel about it.

"We're doing social-emotional learning here," says Gardiner, who used to work for the Canadian Mental Health Association, and who values programs that build a sense of self-worth.

"It used to be you wanted your kids to have a good IQ, but EQ [emotional intelligence] is just as important as IQ," she says.

"So, for kids, if you don't feel good about yourself...you're not going to be successful at school, and if you don't have a full belly you're not going to be concentrating as well when you go to school. So...when the kids come to Veith House during the day, they write their name down on a piece of paper and they put how they're feeling....

"Some of them are happy, some of them will be kind of bored; there's different things that the kids will say, and it's up to them to say what they want to say. And again, if you know how they feel, where they're coming from—if they're sad, or if they're excited for various reasons—it helps you kind of engage them, have a conversation. Or sometimes they might say, 'I'm here and I want to be left alone,' and so you respect that."

❧

MAKING LIVES BETTER

RESPECT IS A huge component of the adult programs, too—respect that many haven't felt much during their lives. Veith

House's programs also offer adults practical ways to make their lives better.

Activities include morning coffee groups, monthly community meals, yoga, and community barbecues that help bring together a clientele that is "socially isolated," Gardiner says. Many are on social assistance, and many experience the anxieties that come with not enough food on the table and not enough money to pay the bills.

Veith House has hosted workshops on money management; in some cases, it directly manages clients' finances through "trusteeships." Clients sign over permission, and social assistance sends their cheques directly to Veith House, whose staff pays their bills; this allows them to rent housing they wouldn't otherwise have.

"People may not be able to get housing anymore because they haven't paid their bills, so a landlord will not rent to them because of their credit history, or the power company will not give them power because they haven't paid their power bill," Gardiner says. With the help of Veith House, clients "can have power and have an apartment and things like that."

Often only "a little bit of spending money" remains, so their financial situations are still precarious. Food insecurity– and the feeling of helplessness that can go along with it–is the biggest source of stress.

"Many clients are on very fixed incomes, and things are getting more and more expensive," Gardiner says, so Veith House helps in other ways.

It's one of the hosts of a mobile food market, which delivers affordable healthy foods to areas like Spryfield,

Fairview, East Preston, and the north ends of Halifax and Dartmouth.

Veith House also provides services its clientele could not otherwise afford—sometimes in innovative ways. It once hosted a free licensed-for-one-day vet clinic. Veterinarians immunized, dewormed, and otherwise treated about fifty animals—everything from cats and dogs to a bearded dragon. Local pet stores donated food.

Veith House has transformed its basement into a massive tool-lending library that looks like a hardware store. Grinders and rotary tools, sanders and electric drills, routers and screwdrivers, and hundreds of other gadgets line the wooden tables, the walls, and the floors below the almost–century-old pipes.

Other rooms, on other floors, are now used for court-ordered supervised visits between children who are under the Province's care and their parents.

Gardiner is always thinking about other ways the building could be used for the betterment of the adults and the children in its midst. "I'm open to trying anything that will help the community, if it's doable and achievable within our ability," she says. "The biggest barrier we have is financial."

Veith House receives core funding from United Way of Canada and from the Nova Scotia Department of Community Services. A number of different charities have also donated everything from food to knapsacks.

On this day, Gardiner has been meeting with a church group about developing a community garden—another piece in the facility's many missions that include feeding bodies and easing minds.

"There's a formal [mental health] system that provides clinical appointments. People go in and see a therapist, and there's a tremendous wait-list for that," Gardiner says. "But there's lots of things people can do to look after their mental health themselves, like going out and standing in a field in the sun....

"There's things like community gardens, and one of the things we're going to do is—we're going to grow a herb garden which will have nice smells and scents, and some of those herbs...when we harvest them, could be things that will make people feel better on the inside, [and they can use them] for making teas and things like that." ·

⁓◦⁓

GIVING PEOPLE A VOICE

IT'S ONE OF the many ways Gardiner hopes to get more people coming to a place that used to be "the best-kept secret in the city."

"I want the doors to be open; I want people to come in," says Gardiner. "More and more, we're just working on how can we make this place more open, more accessible to more people. [We're] listening to people and finding out what they want, and what they need, and what's important to them....

"We're talking about people who sometimes don't have a voice."

On this day, one child's voice is reflected in writing on a whiteboard—on a wall where the girls' dorm used to be.

"Veith House is lit," it says.

Another voice comes from Gardiner's memory—from a woman who's been a client at Veith House and who has faced many struggles, but has found solace in this place that has known both darkness and light.

"This," the woman said, "is the only place I feel like a human being."

Today, other voices echo through the halls and walls as Gardiner makes her way out of the memorial room, heading off to another meeting.

People laugh and talk, and walk down the old wooden stairs.

Outside, a chalkboard sun accompanies an announcement about summer camps for neighbourhood kids.

And the real sun dapples the white picket fence, painted blue and black and green, covered with images of the Halifax

This memorial fence lines one side of the Veith House property today. *(Author photo)*

Explosion, a memorial bell, and monuments and milestones from its history—including the opening of Veith House on July 1, 1970.

The beginning of a new era.

"We're trying to be that soft place to land," Gardiner says. "We're trying to be that safe place."

Chapter Ten: Return

"The past is never dead. It's not even past."

—William Faulkner, *Requiem for a Nun*

T HE HEAT RISES. And a thick haze cloaks the harbour.

Leonard Chater points through the mist and looks to the water.

In the distance, he sees a McDonald's restaurant sign, and beside it, a billboard where the Esso letters used to glow.

Leonard Chater says he's drawn to the building that was once his home. *(Author photo)*

He smiles, thinking about how they once "sparkled" and brightened the nights of two little boys in the shadows.

This is his sixth time returning to the place where he once felt lonely and confused and afraid.

But now, it's like coming "home."

"It draws me," Leonard says, standing in the stillness, looking up at the window where he and his brother Bill used to watch those "beautiful...mesmerizing...colourful lights dancing on the water" while thinking of their mother—"an angel in heaven"—and wondering when she was coming back.

A few weeks after Leonard's visit, Joe Gooey and his wife, Marg, also came back to Veith House—during a sauna of a summer in 2018 when humidity draped the air and memories rose to the surface.

It was Joe's seventh visit.

And like Leonard, he struggled to find the words for the persistent pull of the past, or to explain how fear gave way

Joe Gooey and his wife, Marg, outside Veith House in the summer of 2018. *(Author photo)*

to comfort and became a good memory—compared to his childhood before, and his life after, his time in the institution that had been a staple of the community for more than a century. A place where children had died in the 1800s, and a place where others had lived days and nights as shadowy as the harbour on that summer morning in the heat and the haze.

"Something keeps drawing him here," Marg, Joe's wife, says as they sit in the memorial room—before Joe walks through the building where he had once felt "scared."

And stands by a door where a matron once strapped his back.

And walks along the fence where children once called him "orphan."

And looks up the street where a snowball with a rock almost took his eye.

And still, he says, it was "the nicest place I had ever been."

Other former residents have also come back. But they found little comfort in the revisiting.

Shirley Carter was disappointed when it didn't seem the same as it once had been. For reasons she can't quite explain, she wanted it to be.

Other former residents have never returned. They say they never will.

But either way, what happened to them as children loops through their lives like an old home movie in reverse—replaying moments or feelings or longings in ways big and small, in ways unexpected and understandable.

It's in the teddy bears Shirley—now in her seventies—still collects.

It's in the trains and the toddlers' toys Joe buys for himself.

And it's in the memories that emerge with a touch or a smell, a sound or a colour—no matter the lapses in time or place.

Like the thunder that still makes Linda Gray-LeBlanc take her pillow and go into her bathroom and stay there until it stops.

Or the sadness still comes over Paul Sabarots when he thinks about his life as a boy—"One boy no friends no family just me / Sad and lonely but no one can see."

Earlier that summer, as Joe and Leonard returned to the former orphanage, Paul had just bought a brand-new car and the past returned again—a good memory and a bad memory, rolled into one.

He and his wife, Trudy, were about to drive to Newfoundland in their shiny new Ford Escape Titanium—replete with so many knobs and screens and gadgets, they still hadn't figured out what they were all for.

But Paul had been drawn to the car for another reason. He loved the colour: a beautiful bronze. "Bronze," he said, "has a special place in my heart."

It was the colour of the bike he'd had as a child: a new model Duomatic bronze bicycle that the man he considered his father had bought for him—had paid off over months, on layaway. The first day Paul rode it, some other boys stole it. He eventually hunted them down, beat them up, and got it back—just as he'd fought for so many other things for as long as he could remember.

It takes him back to his earliest memories, summarized in that poem that captures the pain and the fear and the longing of those years in orphanages and foster homes and group homes and a reform school. A poem that, perhaps, captures the emotions of the children who came before him and the children who came after him; children who had, as he'd put it, "No friends no family anywhere / Sad and lonely but no one to care."

He had written these and other verses—"The future is dark and filled with gloom"—when he was thirteen, around the age Joe had been when he'd started working eighteen-hour days on a farm.

And around Linda Gray-LeBlanc's age when she had tried to hide from her abuser in a church.

And around Shirley Carter's age when she had started reading books to other "orphans," hoping that their present and future would be less dark than her own, or others who'd been cast aside by family or fate or other circumstances beyond their control.

He had written them in the time long before they all fought their way out of addiction or mental illness or other obstacles and built successful careers and formed their own families—showing a resolve and a resilience that characterizes the adult lives of many of the orphanage children.

"For me to come from grade seven and teach myself to be able to go in and be a nurse, to be an RN, it takes a lot," Shirley says now. "It's not easy; it's hard studying; it's hard getting there, but you know...the biggest blessing I was given in life is I'm smart....

"God knew I was going to have to be smart because I was going to have a hard time. So I don't look at that as bragging," she says. "It was a gift that was given to me because I was going to have to really work hard."

Joe worked really hard too. He worked his way up in a boiler company and made enough money to buy his own children the kinds of things he'd never had.

Enough to try to fill his own abiding void.

He clicks on his phone and he pulls up pictures—of train sets and wooden ducks. Of gumball machines and Fisher-Price toys—a xylophone and a miniature school bus and happy, plastic, pretend children.

"When I was small, these were the things I wanted," he says, "and I couldn't get them. I like them. I look at them every day."

He often looks at plastic horses too, the kind on the old merry-go-rounds that he used to watch from a distance. He has "lots of those" now, to remind him of the times he walked from the orphanage to the fair and stood there for hours as they, and the other children, circled around and around and around.

"I'd stay up there all day and then I'd come back here and they wouldn't say nothing," he remembers. "Me and my brother, we didn't have [money to go on the rides]. I just watched. I used to like to listen to the music, [to watch] them going around."

Joe says these things without emotion or self-pity, even though his childhood stories sometimes make Marg sad.

"I had my parents, and I had my brothers and sisters. I grew up in a loving family, where he didn't have that," she says. But that makes her even prouder of the man Joe has become.

"He's come a long way. He's really built himself up. He's really succeeded in his life, and so did his brothers and sisters. They really did well for themselves, considering their upbringing."

Joe thinks so too. He repeated grade seven three times, he says, once again. The people he went to school with and the people he laboured for as a child never thought he'd amount to much. But he survived and thrived—learned to figure out just about everything he needed to, on his own.

"I took the roof off my house, did I tell you that?" he wonders. "Then I built a storey on top by myself, no help.

"When you're in my situation—nobody, you had no parents, you had to look after yourself—so if [you] wanted something done, you had to know how to do it."

Shirley understands this. Leonard does too. And they understand the need to create some semblance of a childhood they never had.

Shirley has a room full of teddy bears—exactly how many, she isn't sure. They make her happy. They give her comfort.

"That's because we could never have any," she says.

She couldn't have dolls either, unless the Ladies' Committee came to visit and the matrons let her and the other children hold the toys they weren't allowed to touch at other times. But then took them away as soon as the visitors disappeared.

These days, she likes to give them to others.

"I bought dolls for the kids all the time," she says. "I had a neighbour; I gave her a beautiful doll. I just want people to have dolls—thinking, maybe they need a doll."

But the past still beckons in less comforting ways, too. She still panics when she's in small spaces, or when she smells something musty, or when she sees a cat, or when she thinks of her years as a captive in an adult world. Shirley still needs that extra air.

But something else has happened over the past two years since Shirley—a "private, shut-down person"—shared her story that was for so long "hidden...like it didn't happen."

She's feeling better, she says. It's like a weight has been lifted or a door has been opened.

"Finally, you can let some of it go. It's all tied up in knots in you, and you can let it go."

Every now and then she even lets go of the little fan she normally carries with her from room to room—a small victory toward finding "whatever normalcy" she can.

"I made my life. I became a nurse," she says, proud of the ways she helped herself when no one else would. "And I helped people all my life."

⟳◦⟲

HELPING THEMSELVES

PAUL AND LINDA and Leonard and the others helped themselves too. They had to, when no one else would.

"A lot of the time there wasn't anybody there to lead you along; you had to lead yourself," Leonard says, on that hot summer day near the building that had been both a prison and a haven.

"You had to sort of depend on yourself," he says. "You learned not to lay back and depend on somebody, because a lot of the time they'll let you down."

Lillian, Leonard's wife, says he doesn't let anyone down—this "hardworking, dependable" man; this man of "character" she met in 1972 when she was eighteen, and whom she later married. Together, they raised children who now have children of their own.

They live near their children now in rural Ontario, where she's building a garden and he's got plenty of room to roam, or to fix his neighbours' cars (or to tinker with his own), antiques he taught himself to restore. Now, in retirement, he shows these cars at competitions, where he wins trophies.

"I think it made him a better person," Lillian says of a childhood she still finds "hard to fathom."

"Who can physically slap down somebody tiny with a belt or...a paddle?" she wonders." They were just kids.

"Just kids."

Leonard has made peace with his life as a kid, but reminders remain—like those scars on the inside of his lip from his grandmother's fists.

And the memories of those days and nights at the orphanage without his mom.

He's still trying to unravel some mysteries as time ticks on. He's delved deeply into his family tree—all the way back to England in the 1500s, and to Saint-Pierre and Miquelon in the 1700s, and to Newfoundland, where his ancestors moved and his mother grew up. He's explored the possible parentage of his late sister Anne, who had a different father, and he's still rewinding his own meagre memories of his mom—Jane (Diamond) Chater—with her "curly hair" and her "nice smile." Fragments of those memories make him sad and make him smile.

In one, Leonard and Bill are holding their mother's hand, waiting on the dock for their father.

In another, she's wearing a dress with a black hat and a veil. She pulls it down over her face as she walks out the door.

In his last memory of her, she's on a stretcher in their apartment in Shannon Park. She looks at Leonard, and she smiles—and she becomes "an angel in heaven."

And he becomes "an orphan."

And he watches the lights from the neon letters shining on the harbour—shrouded, sixty years later, in a haze. He's seen them again in his memory—flashing, beautiful, and bright.

And he's seem them again on film—in an old home movie he found on the internet.

It's 1960. A car is driving through Halifax. The day is sunny, but the picture is dark.

The reel clicks and ticks as the car circles the Armdale Rotary and moves along Chebucto Road; travels down North Street and crosses the Macdonald Bridge and passes the incandescent emblem of another time.

The light is red—flickering and lingering, for just a moment.

Before it finally fades away.

Afterword:
The Records Speak

ANNUAL REPORTS and other documents often go into great detail about many mundane aspects of life in the Halifax Protestant Orphans' Home–but leave the issue of the children's welfare largely unexamined. Occasionally, though, they reveal the harsher circumstances inside the institution. They also clearly document provincial funding and the Province's role in sending children to this privately run facility for decades.

ANNUAL SURVEYS

IN THE 1920s, the Province had started funding the orphanage, and it was administering annual surveys–checklists it required all of the institutions it financed to fill out.

The surveys were initiated by long-time—and immensely powerful—public servant Ernest Blois, then—superintendent of what was known as the Office of Neglected and Delinquent Children of Nova Scotia. He ran the provincial department—which had various names, including the Department of Child Welfare and the Department of Public Welfare—for more than three decades, starting in 1912.

The surveys went to all provincially funded orphanages and reform schools, and covered everything from tablecloths and toilets to dining chairs and bathtubs, plus admissions and discharges. They asked for counts on children who were "crippled" or "feeble-minded," or who were "orphans" or "half-orphans"—as those with one living parent were called—and they asked three questions about discipline:

"Are records of punishment kept?"

"Is corporal punishment administered?"

"Is solitary confinement used as punishment?"

Their answers were included in the department director's annual reports, all contained in the yearly Journals of the House of Assembly.

But Brock University historian Renée Lafferty-Salhany, author of *The Guardianship of Best Interests: Institutional Care for The Children of the Poor in Halifax, 1850–1960*, calls the answers "an empty statistic," since Blois didn't require specifics about how children were punished, and didn't try to stop what punishment there was.

Over the years, Lafferty-Salhany says, when asked if there was corporal punishment, "the vast majority of [respondents] said no.

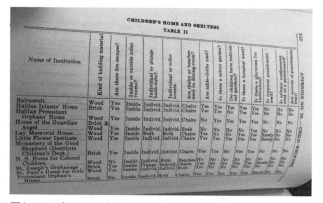

This annual report from 1942 shows the survey questions the Department of Child Welfare asked of various children's institutions. (*Nova Scotia Archives*)

"That doesn't mean they didn't [hurt children]....That happened—no doubt. But they would, on paper, say no," she says.

At the Protestant facility, referred to as both the Halifax Protestant Orphans' Home and the Halifax Protestant Orphanage in Ladies' Committee and provincial reports, answers varied depending on the head matron at the time.

Mrs. Annie Elford, head matron from 1918 to her retirement in late 1937, varied her answers year to year, sometimes admitting to corporal punishment (1921, 1925, 1928) or to "an occasional spanking," (1926) but mostly answering "no" to all three punishment-related questions in Blois's surveys.

Miss Edna Crook, previously an assistant matron, took over the top post, staying until 1944, over the period when the Ontario woman we've called "Margaret" and her little brother lived there. Crook couldn't be located for this book, and it's not clear if she's still living.

For the entirety of her time in the position, Crook answered "no" to all three punishment-related questions.

By 1946, Fred MacKinnon was the director of child welfare, and Sara Patriquin—who lived in the facility with her three daughters—was in charge. Initially, MacKinnon continued the surveys. For two years (1946 and 1947), Patriquin answered "occasionally" when asked if the facility used corporal punishment. She said the home didn't use solitary confinement or keep disciplinary records.

Patriquin continued as head matron until the late 1950s, when she was replaced by Clara McGinn, who stayed until 1965. Patriquin died in 1989.

The surveys continued into the early 1950s. But without explanation, from 1948 on, the discipline questions were no longer asked of the orphanages. They remained in the questionnaires for the reformatories.

꒰꒳ ⊙ ꒰꒳

AUTONOMY

BUT PROVINCIAL FUNDING continued. And so did what Lafferty-Salhany calls the "very autonomous" structure of the children's institutions. Orphanage records and other documents repeatedly make that clear from early on.

"None of the Children's Homes or Shelters are under direct control of the Province," wrote superintendent Blois in his 1925 annual report.

When children are sent to these institutions by the Superintendent or Children's Aid Societies, the statutory grant of $3.00 from the Municipality and $2.00 from the Provincial Treasury, per week, is paid for each child's maintenance.

The Protestant Homes are under the control of private committees or boards of private citizens. The Roman Catholic Homes are managed by the various religious societies, such as the Christian Brothers, the Sisters of Charity, etc.

The details and the amounts of funding changed over time. The orphanage's annual reports and financial records show provincial funding continued to grow as the years passed. Small amounts by today's standards—$1,688 in 1944; $1,439 in 1946—rose to $5,334 by 1957 and more than doubled by 1958 when the provincial government paid most of that year's $28,262 budget, contributing $12,187. That was second only to contributions by privately run—although provincially funded—children's aid societies, at $5,026.

The Province continued to fund the facility annually throughout the 1950s and 1960s—$9,298 in 1960, $7,434 in 1961, $7,771 in 1963—when the average daily cost per child was $2.29 and the annual budget was $30,912.

But the Protestant orphanage continued to operate without direct government supervision even as provincial funding and provincial placement of "wards" grew. This autonomy was the case for most Halifax children's institutions dating back to the early twentieth century, says historian Lafferty-Salhany.

"Nineteenth-century children's homes were privately managed and funded enterprises," she writes in her 2012 book. "Through legal measures, however, the provincial government officially recognized and supported these enterprises and gave their managers the leeway to take charge of poor children, even against the claims of these children's parents. Toward the end of the nineteenth century, some of these institutions received public money to do so; by the end of World War One, all of them did."

The institutions had to take provincial wards or they could lose their provincial funding. The province also required that children be educated, and that the premises remain clean, which could at least partially explain why orphanage documents place such overwhelming emphasis on repairs and cleanliness, as opposed to their treatment of, or the well-being of, the children in their care.

HALIFAX INDUSTRIAL SCHOOL

One institution's shocking disciplinary practices *did* become public.

The Halifax Industrial School was a reform school for boys on Quinpool Road. Founded as The Ragged School in 1850, it became a house of horrors for the children who were sentenced there. Its history paints a picture of deprivation and cruelty that is hard to imagine today, and sheds light on what some institutionalized children faced in the early part of the twentieth century.

Children were sent to the school for actions as minor as begging or skipping school.

In its 1919 report, the school answered "yes" to keeping records and disciplining children. But no one appears to have investigated further or tried to stop the discipline.

Just five years later, in 1924, the *Halifax Citizen* exposed horrific abuses there—forcing a subsequent provincial inquiry, headed by Blois. Children had been repeatedly horsewhipped, choked, beaten with a cat-o'-nine-tails, and dunked headfirst in ice-cold water in winter. They had been handcuffed while beaten; they had been starved; they had been forced to work in dangerous conditions—some even lost limbs as a result. Supervisors forced one child to eat his own stool.

Blois promised reforms. But despite the public scrutiny, the school continued to operate until the late 1940s—and it continued to punish children, as former resident Bill Mont recently recalled.

Mont had been sentenced to five years at the Halifax Industrial School for skipping one day of school in 1938.

> Staff strapped him and forced him and other boys to chop
> wood for kindling; they forced them to sit in silence or
> be punished for speaking. He once witnessed one child
> accidentally chop off the finger of another.

⟡⟡⊙⟡⟡

HUBRIS

THERE'S NO EVIDENCE Blois ever investigated the institutions or orphanages he surveyed, apart from the Halifax Industrial School.

"He was too trusting that those reports were actually giving him a clear picture of the institution," says historian Lafferty-Salhany. "I don't know if that's laziness or complacency or just plain old arrogance—that he just assumed, 'Well, I'm the director; I'm in charge. These women are going to follow my orders and they're going to tell me the truth.' So I think he had probably a great deal of hubris....

"I think that he really truly cared," she adds. "I just think that [it was] his methods, his arrogance, his determination to do things his way—his certainty that what he was doing was perfectly fine, and it wasn't fine. You can't tell the culture of an institution when you're asking about toilets and tablecloths. You can't, unless you talk to the children. That is sort of a modern sensibility he just never explored."

And that was to the detriment of orphanage children—then and later. As adults, almost all of the former residents say that no one ever asked them how they were treated—either in the institutions, or in the foster homes that often followed.

⁓ ◦ ⁓

GLOWING REPORTS

SOMETIMES THE RECORDS offer hints about how children were treated. A fundraising letter, undated, but in archival files for the 1950s and '60s, attempts to place the institution in the best light, even as it casually confirms the use of corporal punishment.

> Children between the ages of three and 12 are received at the home—a large airy building on Veith Street in north Halifax. The entrance to the Home is through a wide entrance hall and the front sitting rooms are flooded with sunshine from tall windows....
>
> In the basement is a spotlessly clean kitchen and across the hall from the kitchen is the dining area. The children pick up their plates and sit at tables for six: two of the older children take care of four of the younger ones. There is a hospital room which is cheerful and bright. For those who are ill there is a television; books, dolls and toys. The children attend Richmond School....Everyone attends Sunday services at St. Mark's Anglican Church. As a matter of fact, they grow up in a

manner just like any other average young child. Bottoms are spanked when necessary. School clothes come off at the end of the afternoon and on go jeans and shirts for play. On rainy days they can use a pavilion; when it's fine there is a big yard at their disposal. Liberal provision is made for the youthful tendency to active play and inside and out there is much space given in which children may exercise muscles as well as minds.

The home's 1960 annual report is one of many that continue to portray an idyllic atmosphere and place a heavy focus on bricks and mortar and decor.

"This past year at the home seems to have been a very happy one," it says.

Mrs. Clara MacGinn [spelled differently here than in other reports] our superintendent, and her staff have worked together to run the home in the most satisfactory manner. Caring for children, especially those who have been deprived of their natural home environment, is a great responsibility and Mrs. MacGinn has not only carried out her duties to satisfaction in this regard, but, has also, with the assistance of her staff, given much time and effort to re-decorating the rooms and a tour through the home these days is an indication of time well spent.

Housekeeping details also take up the bulk of reports during the 1940s and 1950s when former residents say they endured some of the worst abuse. "A salesman has shown [head matron] Mrs. Patriquin some milk mugs that have cleats on the sides, preventing sticking together when piled. They are $3.15 per dozen. Mrs. Patriquin thinks they are worth buying," says a Visitors' Report for July and August 1955

"All five chimneys have been cleaned," notes another from June 1955.

"The curtains in the Isolation room have been washed, lined and rehung," reports an undated account, once again detailing the kind of superficial embellishments which took up so much space in the written records from the beginning of the institution to the end.

꧁ ◉ ꧂

A DARKER REALITY

BUT A DARKER REALITY, mirroring incidents described by former residents, occasionally appears in writing—as in a handwritten account from Ladies' Committee member Carol Roper, dated June 13, 1956.

"On Wednesday, May 30, I called at the orphanage and interrupted a disciplinary session which involved Mrs. Munro and Mrs. Fraser and a nine year old boy," she writes.

This child would not conform and hid under one of the tables, so Mrs. Munro told me—and

according to Mrs. Munro she prodded him out
with a four-foot pole. When I arrived Mrs. Fraser
was standing at the head of the stairs threatening
the child with the same stick. I would recommend
that some action be taken to avoid a repetition as
I felt it was very disturbing to all the children who
witnessed it as well as the child involved.

It isn't clear if the committee took any action or if the "Mrs.
Fraser" mentioned is the long-time cook, whom former
residents almost universally describe as kind—"a doll,"
according to Linda Gray-LeBlanc, who was there in the 1950s.

Later documents show that other matrons—including
then-head matron Clara McGinn—also came under scrutiny.
The Ladies' Committee met on October 29, 1964, to discuss
allegations made by a matron named Ottilie Helene Schmidt.
While some of the references are vague or lack context, they're
similar to the memories of former residents who say they were
beaten, forced to stand for hours, or denied bathroom facilities.

"Mrs. McGinn denied emphatically that any of the children
were 'beaten' and stated that Mrs. Coffin's children and her
own Michael were punished the same as the other children
with denied privileges or spankings as deemed necessary," the
meeting minutes say.

With regard to the statement that the children were
forced to sit or stand inactive, Mrs. McGinn said
this form of punishment [is] used by Miss Schmidt
and not by Mrs. McGinn and not condoned by

Mrs. McGinn. She said that the preschoolers were taken outdoors to play whenever weather permitted.

Mrs. McGinn stated that the bathroom doors upstairs were locked for one hour between 6:00 and 7:00 P.M. when the children ages three to seven were taken up to bed until the older children went to bed. The reason given for locking the bathroom door was that five times in one month plumbers had to be called to remove foreign objects from the toilets....Mrs. McGinn denied that the bathroom doors are locked all night.

Mrs. McGinn does not believe that the children are afraid of her or afraid of any of the matrons. She is of the opinion that Miss Schmidt disliked Michael and the Fagan children and stated that Michael had had his arm injured by Miss Schmidt due to her twisting it. This statement may be verified by a doctor in Chester who examined Michael. Mrs. McGinn spoke to Miss Schmidt about the incident and said she did not wish it to be repeated. The matrons have been instructed by Mrs. McGinn to treat Michael and the Fagan children the same as the other children in the home.

The committee, according its annual report dated May 12, 1965, ultimately dismissed the complaints.

After thorough investigation into the charges, the Executive of the Ladies' Committee recommended to the full Committee that a vote of confidence be given to Mrs. McGinn. This was done in a letter to her. A survey of the Home at this time was conducted by the Dept. of Welfare and they wholeheartedly endorsed the operation.

But, just a few months later, they inexplicably fired the woman they'd previously lavished with praise. As noted in a September 1965 document:

The services of Mrs. Clara McGinn as superintendent of the Halifax Protestant Orphans' Home [have] for some time not been satisfactory.

It is the unanimous opinion of the executive that in the best interest of the home Mrs. McGinn's services be dispensed with and it is therefore recommended to the Ladies' Committee that Mrs. McGinn be dismissed as superintendent of the home effective October 1 and that in lieu of notice her salary be paid by November 1.

The Ladies' Committee voted to fire her, and the September minutes go on to say that "a lengthy discussion followed ranging over many unsatisfactory matters in the home the past two years in particular." It doesn't explain what those matters were.

McGinn could not be located for comment.

❦

"STRUCTURALLY AND FINANCIALLY INDEPENDENT"

SEVERAL REVIEWS OF the Protestant Orphans' Home in the 1960s confirm the Province's role and the facility's apparent autonomy, even in its final years of operation.

"Contact with other agencies seems to have been largely limited to accepting wards for care from Children's Aid Society and the Department of Public Welfare," says a 1966 report from an agency review panel, set up by the then–Halifax-Dartmouth Welfare Council.

"The governing body has been structurally and financially independent of other welfare institutions in the community until very recent years," it adds, noting the orphanage's administrative structure—the all-male board of directors and the Ladies' Committee—appears to be "unique in the Halifax area at this time."

The review found that the orphanage didn't provide any professional services for children or parents; that children slept in "large impersonal dormitories;" and that the playroom was "enormous but appeared bare except for a television placed high on a wall." It suggested that the institution was unable "to provide sufficient attention to meet the emotional needs of each child."

Former resident Linda Gray-LeBlanc, who lived in the orphanage during the 1950s, says most of those matrons certainly weren't qualified to meet the emotional needs of children. "They just hired [people] right off the street," she says.

But the Province continued to place few limits on the orphanage's operations despite these deficiencies and despite its financial support—at least, no documents indicate otherwise.

And that had been the case from the beginning.

Acknowledgements

A BOOK LIKE THIS CAN'T be written without the help of many.

It would not have started without the encouragement of Elaine McCluskey, a writer and editor of tremendous talent and generosity. Thank you, Elaine, for your faith in me and your mentorship.

Many thanks also to Nimbus editor Angela Mombourquette, whose adept editing helped bring this manuscript to completion.

I am grateful to staff at Nova Scotia Archives for their time, patience, and expertise during my long search for orphanage documents.

I am also grateful to *Halifax Magazine* editor Trevor Adams, who first provided a platform for some of these stories.

Thanks to historian Renée Lafferty-Salhany and Dr. Robert Maunder, who brought important historical and psychological context to the book.

And most importantly, I want to thank all the former residents of Halifax Protestant Orphans' Home who, despite their often-painful recollections, were willing to share their childhood memories with me.

Note on Sources

THE MATERIAL IN this book is drawn partly from documents held at the Nova Scotia Archives; other material was drawn from my interviews with former residents of the Orphans' Home and others.

Many photos were generously provided by the people who told their stories here. Others are from the Nova Scotia Archives, and the rest I took myself.

DURING HER LONG newspaper career, Lois Legge wrote hundreds of feature stories, including profiles of Holocaust survivors, war veterans, and famed photographer Robert Frank. Lois has won three Atlantic Journalism Awards and has been nominated ten times. She's a two-time National Newspaper Award finalist. Lois lives in Dartmouth, N.S., with her husband, Richard. They have one daughter, Chelsea.